BAC LIGHTNING

Previous page: Humidity was high at the Farnborough show in 1968 when this unusual picture of an F6 in Saudi markings was taken, hence the mist effect as the aircraft makes a high-speed pass. A camera pack protrudes from the underbelly. / *Brian M. Service*

Below: Turning night into day. A No 74 Squadron F1 runs up its Avons on reheat, its tiger's head tail badge illuminated by the parking stand floodlights. / *BAe*

BAC LIGHTNING
Modern Combat Aircraft 5

Arthur Reed

LONDON

IAN ALLAN LTD

Acknowledgements

The author wishes to acknowledge with gratitude the help which he received in researching this book from very many people connected with British aviation, in particular Trevor Tarr (without whose tireless and enthusiastic support the project would never have, 'left the runway') and Wing Commander R. P. Beamont, both of British Aerospace.

Arthur Reed

London,
January 1979

First published 1980

ISBN 0 7110 0988 0

Published by Ian Allan Ltd, Shepperton, Surrey; and printed in the United Kingdom by Ian Allan Printing Ltd

Contents

Left: Togetherness. Four No 11 Squadron F6s, armed with Red Top, in close up formation. The squadron took on the training responsibility on Lightnings from the autumn of 1975. / *MoD via P. Collins*

A Classic Fighter

The English Electric (now British Aerospace) Lightning will go down in the history of aviation as one of the most classic of fighters. It was the first and only truly supersonic aircraft to be fully developed by Britain on her own, and as such it was beloved by pilots, but not so enthusiastically received by politicians. Its story covers three decades (the 1950s, 1960s and 1970s) and parts of two more (the latter part of the 1940s, and very likely the whole of the 1980s) so that it is at once both an historical aircraft and one that remains very contemporary.

Its conception occurred very shortly after the end of World War II when English Electric, who had come back into aviation in 1938 and had spent the war years making aircraft from other companies' designs, looked round for new designs of their own. They started the Canberra bomber which, although it turned out to be one of the best British sellers, was, with its straight wing and its two engines placed in the wings — a similar layout to that tried in the Meteor fighter — no great technical breakthrough.

The Lightning, however, was, 'something else' as sketched on the back of the proverbial envelope — a 60° sweepback wing, two engines mounted one on top of the other inside a slab-sided fuselage, with the pilot sitting on top of the lot, advanced avionics which would turn the aircraft into a flying platform for shooting down with missiles enemy bombers, an all moving tail, and powered controls. Such an advanced design was hard to swallow at the Ministry of Supply and at the Royal Aircraft Establishment, Farnborough, but the Ministry swallowed it sufficiently to issue in 1947 an experimental study contract, ER103, and then two years later a contract, F23/49, for two prototypes and an airframe to be used for static test.

Right: First flight of the P1, the original prototype, took place at Boscombe Down on 4 August 1954, Boscombe being preferred to the English Electric company airfield at Warton by the test pilot, Wg Cdr R. P. 'Bee' Beamont because of the longer runway. One of the pair of Sapphire engines shoots flame during a run-up prior to flight. / *British Aerospace (BAe).*

What EE were building up to produce in the period when World War II had been over less than five years was an aircraft which constituted a quantum leap forward in design and which would be capable of speeds up to 1,500mph. It was a remarkable push against the frontiers of technology, when it is remembered that the first jet aircraft, the Meteor, went to RAF squadrons just before the end of the war, and the second, the Vampire, in 1946. The speed of the Meteor F1 was 385mph, of the Meteor F4 585mph, and of the Vampire 540mph. Only seven years before English Electric won their experimental study contract in 1947 the biplane Gloster Gladiator had been in front-line service with the RAF with a top speed of 253mph.

The team producing the Lightning design was generally very young and some of them had little experience of designing aircraft. RAE Farnborough obviously felt there was call for a belt-and-braces exercise, saying that the 60° wing sweep proposed was too revolutionary, and that lesser sweeps ought to be tried. A test aircraft, the Short SB5, was therefore ordered into development, but all this proved was that the EE men had in fact got it right, and a quarter of a century later, those who were involved in the comparison at English Electric sum up the SB5 experiment as a waste of time and public money.

First flight of the P1 Lightning WG760 was made on 4 August 1954. In its lines it was an experimental vehicle and very different to the aircraft which eventually went to the RAF squadrons. Improvements, including the replacement of Sapphire engines with Avons, a centrebody in the engine intake to enable the aircraft to reach higher Mach numbers, and a raised cockpit were introduced and the resulting aircraft became the P1B. A contract for three P1Bs to be the prototypes for the RAF fighter was given to English Electric in 1954. The first of these, XA847, was flown for the first time on 4 April 1957 — the very day that the Conservative Government of the day published its White Paper forecasting the end of manned aircraft and their replacement by missiles.

Several other British military aircraft projects were cancelled in this period, but the Lightning survived. The first production aircraft made its maiden flight on 29 October 1959, by which time the Rolls-Royce Avon 210 with reheat to give a maximum thrust of around 14,300lb, and the AI23 radar linked to Firestreak missiles had been developed. Deliveries to the RAF began in December of that year, and with home orders well under way, British Aircraft Corporation, which in 1960 had English Electric merged into it, began to think of ways in which their fighter's export potential could be exploited.

Unfortunately, the basic concept of the Lightning had always been as a short-dash interceptor. It had the remarkable ability of an initial climb of 50,000ft in 60sec but once at altitude and accelerating to 1,500mph it had only sufficient fuel to make one pass on an enemy aircraft before having to return to base to refuel. Potential buyers in the export market were interested in the Lightning as a ground-attack aircraft, and for this role it needed far more fuel than was originally designed in. But in 1963 the government authorised BAC to develop a long-range version of the Lightning, mainly so that it could be ferried out to distant theatres of war, such as Singapore and Cyprus. This led to the Lightning Mark F6 which had a new tank built into an area-ruled bulge beneath the fuselage and in which the flaps had been made capable of carrying fuel. The aircraft finished up with a range 40% better than earlier Lightning marks, as well as multi-role capability, and as such it was sold, in 1965 to Saudi Arabia in what was described at that time as the country's biggest-ever export deal. Kuwait also bought the Lightning a little later.

The sad fact was that had these improvements been sanctioned earlier, the Lightning might well have been sold to a much longer list of export clients, and in particular the NATO nations, several of which seriously considered the type before buying American Lockheed F-104 Starfighters. As it was the Lightning's only operator on a large scale was the RAF, with which Service it served largely in West Germany as part of the British NATO contribution, and as part of the UK home defence. The bulk of the Lightning squadrons was phased out of RAF service in the mid-1970s, but two squadrons will remain based in England until at least the early 1980s and possibly to the end of that decade.

Left: The cambered leading edge which was introduced into the P1 in 1956-57 to improve its cruising range can be seen clearly in this picture. The modification was incorporated in the Mark 6 and Mark 2A Lightnings for the RAF and the Marks 53 and 55 for Saudi Arabia and Kuwait. / *BAe via R. P. Beamont*

Above: Airborne! On one of the early test flights, Bee brings the P1 WG760 in close to the Meteor which was being used as a photographic/chase aircraft. / *BAe*

Right: Bee takes a nostalgic look at the cockpit which was his airborne 'office' during hundreds of test flights as the development programme progressed from P1 into the fully-fledged Lightning. / *BAe*

9

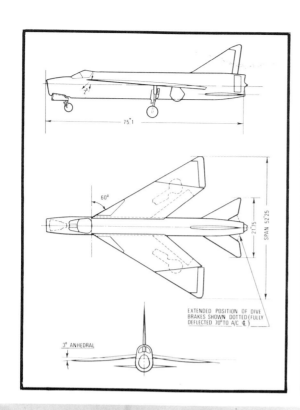

60°

75·1

SPAN 5·225

21·75

EXTENDED POSITION OF DIVE
BRAKES SHOWN DOTTED (FULLY
DEFLECTED 70° TO A/C ℄)

3° ANHEDRAL

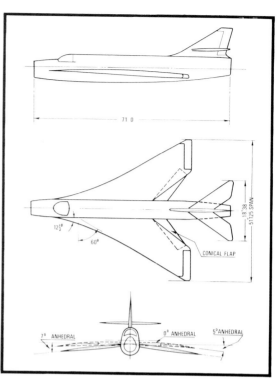

71·0

18·38
5·125 SPAN

12½°

60°

CONICAL FLAP

7° ANHEDRAL   0° ANHEDRAL   5° ANHEDRAL

Far left and left: High tail or low tail. This was the debate which exercised the minds of the men designing what was to become the Lightning and which resulted in many 'back-of-envelope' sketches, two of which are reproduced here. That with the tail low down is more nearly representative of the aeroplane which was produced. The high-tail format in the other sketch shows a more 'streamlined' wing, the rear of which begins to look like a delta with the fillet partially filled in by conical flaps. This tail position was backed by the Royal Aircraft Establishment, but was proved unstable in tests with a specially-built experimental aircraft, the Short SB5.

Below left: In this posed publicity still, the lines of the P1 can be seen as very different to the Lightning which eventually went to the RAF. Main external differences were in the design of the fin and the replacement of the 'fish-mouth' air intake with a more circular shape containing a centre-body holding the radar. / *BAe*

Below: Transonic shock waves can be seen coming off of this model Lightning as it 'flies' at Mach 0.98 in one of the English Electric wind tunnels (see photo p83). / *BAe via M. Hooks*

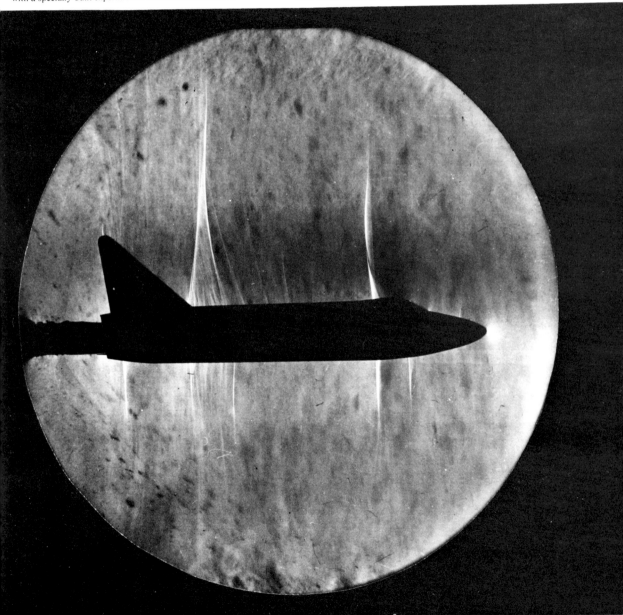

11

Political Intervention

Like virtually every military aircraft which has been developed in Britain since World War II, progress of the Lightning was bedevilled by politics to such an extent that its true potential was never truly realised. The fact that it was conceived at all was surprising, for in the middle 1940s British aviation was still labouring under the misconceived policy from government that supersonic flight was too dangerous for test pilots and that any trials should be carried out through the use of models dropped from subsonic aircraft.

This policy had led to the cancellation of a project for a supersonic research aircraft, the Miles M52. It was a quaint decision on a par to the advice to Queen Victoria at the beginning of the railway age that to travel at speeds in excess of 30mph would be likely to cause fatal damage to the royal personage. Fortunately, there were plenty of British test pilots who were ready to take their chance above Mach 1, and also fortunately there was the English Electric design team at Warton, Lancashire, who were farsighted enough to see that there was no doubt that aviation progress had no alternative but to pass through the sound barrier.

They were at once bolstered by the knowledge that in the United States the first (the X8-86) of what was to be a whole series of new aircraft projects, some of them with radically-swept wings, was appearing capable of exceeding the speed of sound without killing pilots in the process. But in spite of this evidence, there was scepticism in certain quarters of government and the Civil Service as to whether the future of military aviation really lay in manned supersonic flight; many believed that not only would it be too dangerous, and certainly too costly, but that it would be superseded by missiles before it achieved anything.

These doubts showed themselves in the way in which permission to proceed on the Lightning was eked out to English Electric by the government departments concerned, but the project also proceeded at a slow pace because of the basic decision agreed between government and manufacturers to take the step into supersonic aviation with great care and to build a large number of prototypes — 20, in fact — so that the many and varied parts of the new aircraft could be thoroughly tested. A much larger effort on supersonics in the United States had resulted in a whole string of new projects test-flying, with the result that there was far less reliance on large numbers of prototypes, and the first production aircraft came off of the assembly lines much more quickly.

The situation was summed up in a remarkably frank background note issued by English Electric during 1963 which recalled that due to the particularly cautious attitude prevailing in authoritative circles during the immediate postwar era, Britain lagged sadly behind in supersonic flight for a period of several years. In fact, EE recalled, it was not until the prototype P1 exceeded Mach 1 in level flight in 1954 that the first true supersonic flight took place in Britain (this was the third flight of the P1, on 11 August 1954, from Boscombe Down). The 1957 Defence White Paper had been, EE said, 'popularly, but wrongly' interpreted as meaning the end of the manned fighter, and chopping off all development of supersonic aircraft. This was the epoch of the Lightning and it was sometimes overlooked that the achievement of a Service aeroplane not only of Mach 2 performance, but of Mach 2 as a fully-integrated weapons system with conjointly developed navigation, radar, armament, and fire-control equipment of advanced technique, was attained in a single step compared with, for instance, the United States' overall research programme which employed several different experimental and development aircraft over separate progressive stages.

An operational supersonic aircraft required about three times the amount of engineering man-hours to design and develop as a corresponding, high-speed subsonic aeroplane of equal basic weight, and the amount of flight testing necessary to explore its performance and prove the functioning of its diverse equipment would extend indefinitely into the future if the older methods of using one or two prototypes were employed. EE explained that for the Lightning programme, the Ministry of Aviation had authorised the manufacture of a development batch of 20 aircraft, each being allotted a specific task in the overall flight testing programme, 'so that different aspects of performance and equipment functioning could be explored at the same time without one being dependent on the progress of the other.'

Right: In the Warton circuit in 1958 is the prototype T4 flown by Bee. This same aircraft was lost on 1 October 1959 through what is assumed to have been a fin failure (although security blankets the actual cause to this day). Johnny Squier, test pilot on that occasion, ejected safely, but spent over 28 hours in the Irish Sea before being rescued. / *BAe via R. P. Beamont*

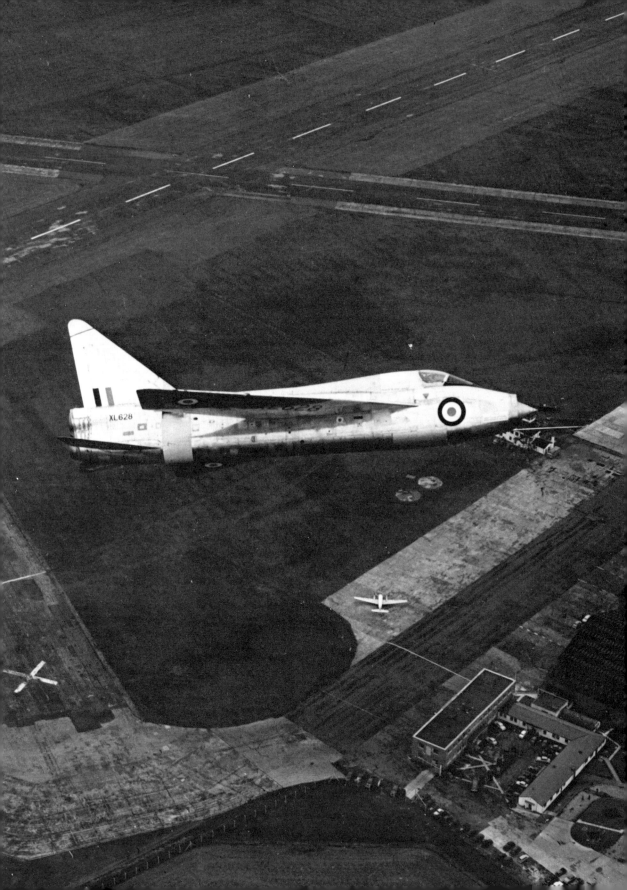

By 1963, more than 5,000 test flights had been made since the P1 first flew in 1954. Of these, 4,000 were at supersonic speeds. But even the test flying was subject to a certain amount of political interference, and the environmental lobby was beginning to form to protest about the new phenomenon of the sonic boom which the Lightning produced on the ground as it went about its supersonic test programme. As EE said at the time, special problems arose in supersonic flight testing, not least of which were those due to covering the ground at 20-25 miles/min when a rate 1 turn could encompass the best part of the county of Lancashire, or the equivalent sea area, in a few minutes, and when radar controlled avoiding action with other civil or military air users had to be initiated while the aircraft were still 20 miles apart.

At these speeds, a small navigational error — a normal VHF fix could take two minutes, by which time the aircraft was about 50 miles further on — or too wide a turn at the end of a sea run, brought rapid contact with the Press, police, local authorities and the public at large: 'as the always-present trailing air disturbance manifests itself over land with the readily-identified sonic bang.' Extensive mechanical testing and electronic simulator work, and wind-tunnel testing was employed before and during the Lightning flight-test programme, English Electric said. There were both wind and water tunnels at Warton, and the newer Mach 4 and Mach 6 tunnels were the fastest in Europe. During the Lightning programme, 51 accurate scale models were made, and more than 4,600 wind tunnel runs were carried out. The attitude of the authorities towards the testing of Britain's new supersonic fighter was not always as helpful as it might have been, and when the aircraft went for tests on the government firing ranges, BAC discovered that they had to pay the government £1,000 every time a Lightning fired its guns or missiles.

This state of affairs was brought to light in September, 1967 by Mr Alec Atkin, Lightning project manager, during a visit by the Press to the Warton factory to have the first sight of the variable geometry aircraft which Britain was proposing to build following the collapse a few months earlier of the Anglo-French VG project. I wrote in *The Times* at that time that firing tests by the Lightning took a few seconds, and the Lightnings were over the ranges for no more than 10 minutes at a time. Test firings had to be made at least once a week over the previous six months, which meant that BAC had run up a bill of about £25,000 for trials of an aircraft which they were trying to sell abroad for the good of Britain.

Mr Atkin also waxed strong on that occasion on the overall government role in the Lightning project, saying that the fact that the RAF had only this one type of supersonic aircraft in service was a discredit to

successive governments, to the air staff, and to the industry. The potential of the Lightning had not been fully exploited. BAC had suggested in 1957 developing it in various roles. If these had been accepted, Britain would have saved a lot of imports of American aircraft, and would have had a greater export potential.

Inevitably, the Ministry of Technology came up with a justification of the charges which they levied for providing range services. It was not, the ministry said, just a question of flying over the range for 10 minutes. There was much more to it than that — all sorts of complicated services and instrumentation had to be provided for such tests. Total cost was not worked out until all the trials had taken place, and until then any figures for a single test must just be an estimate: 'As public money is involved, we have to charge realistic prices for the services provided.' Interviewed in January 1979, Mr Atkin, now Managing Director (Military) of British Aerospace said:

'BAC frequently put forward developments for the Lightning from its inception in the early 1950s. However, due to defence policies, the primary role seen for the Lightning for the early 1960s was that of an interceptor, as a defence deterrent, in the UK. No interest was expressed by the Ministry of Aviation in extending the number of roles of the Lightning any further. Indeed, the policy of development for the interceptor role only was taken to the extent that the guns that had been basic to the fits of the early marks of Lightning were removed as being unnecessary in the interceptor role, and the requirement was then to integrate the Lightning, in its defence of the deterrent role, into a sophisticated air defence system of a largely-automated ground environment, the medium/high altitude surface-to-air missile system, and the Lightning force.

'Shortly after the development of the Mark 3 Lightning, a further change of defence policy saw the Lightning once again in the dual role of interceptor and air superiority fighter, and a requirement was raised once again to restore guns in the aircraft for the air superiority role, and also to increase the combat fuel. This was accomplished on the Mark 6 Lightning

Above right: On an appearance, probably in 1957, over its home airfield at Warton, the P1 does a tight turn around the new English Electric control tower. By that time the cambered leading edges had been fitted. / *The Times*

Right: English Electric's breakthrough in fighter technology inevitably brought a succession of VIPs to the door at Warton, among them Duncan Sandys, who as Conservative Minister of Defence in 1957, produced the White Paper which predicted that manned fighters would be replaced by missiles. Despite this wild prophesy, the Lightning project survived. Sandys is centre right, wearing waistcoat and watchchain. / *BAe*

by the addition of a ventral fuel tank and gun-pod combination. At this stage we would also have wished to have endowed on the Lightning the capability for the Sparrow missile when it came into service with the USAF, which we believed would have provided a significant improvement in the interceptor role. This also would, perhaps, have frustrated the requirement for the Phantom in the interceptor role in the Royal Air Force.

'There is no doubt that as a flying machine, the Lightning is superb and performs splendidly well even by present day standards some 25 years after it was

first flown. We spent a lot of time in getting that right and there was not a lot we could have done to develop those aspects any further.

'As it was, we aspired greatly to sell the Lightning in the export market and, therefore, we decided to invest as a company in extending the roles in which the Lightning could be used. The further development of the guns, the air-to-ground weapon system, and carriage of weapons such as bombs and rockets, as well as an imaginative and very effective reconnaissance facility proved to be invaluable in selling the Lightning to both the Royal Saudi Air Force and the Kuwait Air Force.'

The blinkered thinking which was apparent in the Ministry of Technology over charging for firing tests was mirrored in the Ministry of Defence over the manner in which the Lightning was to fulfil its role as an interceptor. While the Americans were concentrating on developing a radar attack system combined with missiles which could catch an enemy from whichever direction the fighter approached, the British plan was to continue the traditional 'stern chase', and the missiles which were ordered into development for the Lightning had to lock on to the jet efflux of the intruder.

The doubts which had been rumbling around in Whitehall about the future of manned aircraft erupted in the 1957 Defence White Paper, introduced by the then Secretary of State for Defence, Mr Duncan Sandys. Entitled, *Defence— An Outline of Future Policy*, the document included the phrase which has gone down in British aviation history that: 'in view of the good progress already made, the Government have come to the conclusion that the RAF are unlikely to have a requirement for fighter aircraft of types more advanced than the supersonic P1, and work on such projects will stop.' The Lightning project had slipped through the net because it was well advanced by that time and because its major use was in the defence of Great Britain at heights of 40,000-50,000ft. But few people in Whitehall gave it much of a career, the thinking being that it would be superseded before it had been in service for very many years by the robot air army envisaged in the Sandys defence document.

This thinking resulted in Whitehall becoming unprepared to spend very much on developing and improving a product which, they believed, would be bound for the scrapheap shortly. By 1958, English Electric had prepared a design for an improved version of the Lightning, with an eye firmly on the export market. It had an improved wing and a much-improved fuel capacity which, with a wide range of options on offensive weapons, made it an ideal ground-attack aircraft. West Germany was an interested potential customer, but there was no support, and even opposition in this sphere for the Lightning from the government, and English Electric, who were fully stretched in funding successfully export versions of the Canberra, had no money left over for private funding of their supersonic fighter.

Had West Germany bought the Lightning there is not much doubt that some of the other NATO nations would have followed suit so that overall sales could have reached the 1,000 mark. Government also squashed at this time a plan to fit Lightnings with a rocket booster to assist the performance at high altitudes where, because of the thin air, thrust falls away and fuel consumption rises if reheat is used to keep up the speed. A Double Scorpion rocket had been used on a Canberra to attain for that aircraft a world height record of 70,310ft on 28 August 1957, and in February the following year it was announced that a similar device was to be fitted to the P1B (although provision for it had been designed in from the start). Alas, the idea came to nothing.

The shadow cast by the 1957 defence policy statement hung over the Lightning, and indeed over

the whole aerospace industry in Britain until the early 1960s, by which time it was beginning to become obvious that the premise that missiles were to take over from manned aircraft was in fact nonsense. TSR2 was started up, only to be cancelled in 1967 on the grounds of cost, and in the United States and the Soviet Union new marks of fighters and bombers, all with cockpits to accommodate human beings, were rolling off the production lines. The RAF accepted that there was scope for improved versions of the Lightning, its engines and its attack system, but it was still difficult to obtain funds for such developments from the Treasury.

Such parsimony helped to lead to the scrapping of the auto-attack system which had proved in flight trials that Lightnings could search out and lock on to an enemy, and be flown right into battle without the pilot actually touching the controls. Then, in 1963, came the dramatic reversal of policy in Whitehall which accepted that manned fighters had a future after all. BAC were officially informed by government that the Lightning was short on range and authorisation was given to develop it as a long-range aircraft — which in turn led to the sales to both Saudi Arabia and Kuwait.

In all, the Lightning development programme strung out over a total of 15 years and produced six different versions for the RAF, plus two export versions. This protracted story had much to do with dilly-dallying on the political front, but delays were also produced simply because the Lightning did represent such an enormous jump in technology, so that its design, testing and development had to be accompanied by a new series of procedures for specifying and evaluating in which progress along the learning curve proceeded only very slowly. Development times and costs inevitably escalated in this unexplored environment, but all of these 'growing pains' could be considered as an investment by Britain in future supersonic aircraft projects and helped to ensure the effectiveness decades later of such aircraft as the Jaguar and the Tornado.

As an ironical footnote, it was the Lightning which was enlisted by the Labour Government in 1967 to test public reaction to the most brilliant jewel in the technological crown of the British aircraft industry, the Concorde supersonic airliner — as a result of which tests, the Concorde's chances of becoming a commercial success were, to say the least, not helped. Lightnings from the RAF squadrons were ordered to make a series of sonic booms above London and the other major cities in Britain and the public were asked to write in to give their reactions. The tests were widely publicised, and the reaction was vociferous — sometimes so vociferous that booms were reported on days when the Lightnings had remained in their hangars. But as a result of these tests, the Government became convinced that the Concorde flying over land supersonically would not be acceptable, and the case against the supersonic aircraft was immeasurably strengthened.

Author's note: During my researches for this book I found some senior people in the British aircraft industry who opined that the real reason why Whitehall did not sanction the full development of the Lightning was that they wanted Britain to buy Phantoms from the United States. This in fact happened in February 1965, and the RAF eventually took 118 Phantoms into service. Each was 'Anglicised' to the extent of 45%, the main changes being the introduction of a Ferranti inertial nav/attack system, and Rolls-Royce Spey engines, the latter modification proving a lengthy and expensive task.

Below left: Members of the English Electric ground staff put the final touches to the P1 at Warton before it is towed out for disposal at the end of its useful life. / *BAe*

Below: The definitive version; the Mark 6 first production aircraft banks away from the air-to-air camera over the Lake District during test flying in 1964. / *BAe via R. P. Beamont*

Early Days

The Lightning was 'born' in a garage in the centre of Preston, Lancashire, which had been acquired a few years earlier by English Electric for the team which designed the Canberra. There, the chief engineer of the EE aviation division, W. E. W. 'Teddy' Petter, led a team of eager young men talented in all the various sectors of aircraft design and development, many of whom went on to occupy senior positions in the management of the nationalised aircraft industry, British Aerospace.

In addition to Petter, the leading members of that team were, Ray Creasey, chief aerodynamicist, Dai Ellis, chief of flight test and wind tunnels, Harry Harrison, chief production engineer, F. W. Page, chief of stress, and Wing Cdr R. P. 'Bee' Beamont, chief test pilot. Beamont remained the Lightning project pilot with sole responsibility for the flight testing evaluation programme from 1948 until his last Lightning test flight in 1968 — a remarkable record. The closeness of this flight development group, and in particular the belief by both Petter and subsequently Page in the continuous integration of the test pilot with the designers from the beginning, is undoubtedly one of the major reasons why the P1 and the developments which followed it always had such excellent flying qualities, despite the fact that so many technological boundaries were being crossed at one time.

The first prototypes were virtually hand-crafted at the EE works at Warton airfield, but then production of the major sections shifted to the EE works in the centre of Preston and at Accrington. The large sections were taken by road to the EE airfield at Samlesbury, not far from Warton, where the final assembly line was established. The first flight of each aircraft was from Samlesbury to Warton, from which airfield (apart from the first flight and some early operations from the Government test establishment at Boscombe Down) all of the test flying took place.

Sir Frederick Page, now chairman of the BAe commercial aircraft division, took over the leadership of the design team when Petter left EE to go to Folland to oversee the development of the Gnat trainer. He recalled:

'At the time the team at English Electric was very busy with the Canberra, an immense programme, and it was a very advanced aeroplane for its time. It was a distillation of the best practice from all over the world, although it followed fairly conventional lines. There was a lot of debate going on about what the aircraft policy of the country should be, some of it on what our supersonic aircraft policy should be. The general view was that we had got a ten-year thinking interval and that some things were likely to be too difficult. The Miles M52 supersonic aircraft project was cancelled in 1946 because it was felt by some government advisers that, at least for the time being, supersonic flight was one of the "too difficult" things. The basic research was going to be done instead by dropping models from aeroplanes.

'In English Electric we were fortunate. One generally finds that there are some enlightened people in government and in industry and these people reached some positive agreement on the future of supersonic flight in Britain starting as a design study ER103 in 1947, which turned into F23/49, which in turn led to the P1A/P1B and thus the Lightning. English Electric put in some money to back it and got some funding from HMG. Doubts remained among some people — not us — about the difficulty of supersonic flight, but some very courageous work had been done by one of the RAE pilots in a Spitfire in straight-down dives. Very little was known at that time about control and stability and about what happened to air-flow at around Mach 1. The background was therefore one of uncertainty and we were wondering what we were going to do next.

'We had a number of very bright people and we put our heads together and gathered all the information we could from various sources, including Germany, where they had got quite a long way during the war with high-speed wind tunnel tests and with high-speed aircraft. The Americans were doing some very early experimental work backed by a tremendous amount of research in tunnels. We put all these together and came to the conclusion that, although it might be difficult, we ought not just to be thinking of supersonic projects but actively starting them.

'We decided to make an investment in supersonic research. We did not have any large contracts for supersonic work at that time but we had always put a fair amount of money back in the business to sustain the long-term. One of the things we decided to do was to build a transonic/supersonic wind tunnel but, as a

Right: The ultimate SB5 wing sweep position of 69° and the tail in the low position made it into something close to a delta. / *Shorts*

private company, we could not afford a vast facility so we bought some old Nene engines which were scrapped as far as airborne use was concerned but were good for use on the ground, and we built an induced-flow wind tunnel; it was one of the first of its kind for transonic/supersonic testing in this country. Serious thinking started early in 1947, decisions were taken in 1947/48 and the tunnel started running in 1949/50.

'There was a German working at RAE, who had worked in the German industry during the war, who was starting to convince people that supersonic flight was really practicable. People began to modify the original view that supersonic flight was too difficult to a view that, although there were problems, they were not insuperable. Things jelled by 1949 with the issue of specification F23/49 and we aimed to make a quantum jump with what was ultimately to become the Lightning. The Canberra was then the optimum subsonic aeroplane and we aimed to progress in one jump from that stage to Mach 2, and I suspect that you would be pushed to find any other company in the world who did that jump –– most of them made several intermediate steps.

'We took an existing engine, although we would have liked one which was specifically designed for supersonic performance, and we did get quite a way down the road in discussing such an engine with Rolls-Royce, but it was felt that the country couldn't afford it and it was too difficult technically, so we had to make do at various stages in the programme with whatever engines were available. Reheat experience in this country, at that time, was very limited and we used a fixed system to make it as cheap and simple as possible in the original experimental vehicle — which was the P1A; but it did enable us to test a basic concept, which was a wing with a 60° sweep and a few other novel ideas.

'We wanted a high sweep because all the tunnel tests indicated that that was the configuration which gave the optimum supersonic performance with the power plants available, and which were likely to be available in the future, and would permit the use of a reasonably thick wing section for stowage of fuel while leaving the fuselage free to stuff in as much thrust as we could possibly get. The reason for the wing shape was that we wanted to achieve very good lateral control and all available data showed that the aileron hinge line should be at right angles to the line of flight. This did cut down slightly on performance but we did get very good control. We also wanted good longitudinal control and tunnel-tested the tail in various positions, from T-tail, to the bottom of the fuselage.

'We soon found that the high tail produced pitch-up, which would have been disastrous under any circumstances and particularly in combat. As we dropped the tail things got better and we came to the conclusion that it had to be well below the plane of the wing. In that position we achieved excellent control and stability and could get away with quite a small all-moving tailplane without elevators. This decision caused a certain amount of fuss and bother among some people on the basis that no one had put tailplanes below the level of the wing in the past and it was going to be very difficult for anybody to support anything so revolutionary. At that time, I had to go to the United States and took the opportunity to visit some of the research establishments there. They said that they had come to the same conclusions that we had.

'Despite that, a totally unnecessary exercise was begun which resulted in a research aircraft called the Short SB5, "to see if these guys at English Electric were right or wrong". We said that one only had to look at the tunnel tests and apply some elementary reasoning and then check with the Americans, who were coming to the same conclusions. A little later the French reached the same conclusion that a low tail was the answer with their Espadon aircraft. Shorts did their work extremely loyally with us but it need never have been done; it took up time and was misleading because the SB5 could never be properly representative.

'For example, we had another revolutionary idea, for those days, which was that if the aeroplane was to handle well as a fighter regardless of speed, whether subsonic, transonic or supersonic, all the controls had to be fully-powered, duplicated and with artificial "feel" built in. Moreover, the all-moving tailplane without elevators could obviously not be moved by hand and was designed to be operated by fully-powered, twin-screw jacks. A few bold decisions like that inevitably meant that we could not build a quick, cheap and simple test aircraft.

'One small thing came out of the SB5 which gave us advance warning of a problem, but it was nothing to do with the primary purpose for which that aeroplane was built. There was lateral rocking at circuit speeds which pilots did not like. We looked at the flow pattern over the wing in the wind tunnel and found that the lateral rocking was due to irregular breakdown of flow as between one wingtip and the other. We thumbed through all the available information on flow patterns on the tips of high-speed wings and concluded that a device on which the Americans had done tests, and had then shelved, was the answer. This was a small "notch" in the leading edge of the wings. We put it on the aeroplane and it worked like a charm, and it was also used to house the vent for the fuel system. Some time later the Americans asked "How did you think of that notch?" We said, "We just thumbed through your research reports."

'The Lightning also contained a number of other ideas that were novel at the time the decisions had to be taken, although they are now generally accepted practice. The electrical system generated stabilised, high-voltage AC power instead of low-voltage DC. There was an elementary form of head-up display tied into the radar and other sensors. The autopilot was not only coupled to the instrument landing system to provide auto-approach, but also incorporated auto-throttle control.

'When you consider the quantum jump that we made with the Lightning, we could easily have got things a lot less right than we did. Unfortunately, just when we ought to have been capitalising on our early decisions the Sandys White Paper came out saying virtually that manned fighters had no future and that missiles would take over. This was the most disastrous document ever produced because it stopped future development in its tracks. We are still suffering from it, and, although good, our export effort has been hampered by an artificial throttle being put on it which no one else had.'

Mr A. N. Rhodes and Mr I. C. Taig, both of whom were stressmen, said that the Lightning wing posed special problems to the designers:
'There were no known stressing methods for a structure with a 60° sweep and totally new methods had to be developed. In the early days we used a manual method, known as "relaxation", which required 12 months of effort by three or four people to obtain a solution. By 1951-52 we were able to make some use of a computer: the ACE at the National Physical Laboratory developed in conjunction with

Right: Another VIP at a later stage was Julian Amery, who as a Conservative Minister was a great supporter of the British aircraft industry, and particularly the Concorde supersonic airliner. He is seen being helped into a two-seater Lightning by test pilot Johnny Squier prior to a ride. / *BAe*

Below: The lads from the hangar and the technical office are assembled to pose in front of the P1, which is wearing its 'fencer's mask' air intake blank. In the group are (ninth from right) F. W. Page, who led the development team, and, 11th from right, test pilot Beamont. / *BAe*

the English Electric Company. We needed to determine the stress distribution in the wing so that the structure could be designed to take the internal loads. This was the first time that a computer had been used for this type of stress analysis in the UK and possibly in the western world.

'The capacity of the computer was no more than that of a mini computer today. In aircraft with wings at right angles to the fuselage it had always been assumed that the principal bending loads would be at right-angles to the direction of flight and distributed according to classical bending theories. With a 60° sweep there was a concentration of stress towards the rear of the wing, which was known to be severe but which could not be calculated by existing methods.

'We took up some work that had been done by Prof Nicholas Hoff at the Polytechnic Institute of Brooklyn for the National Advisory Committee for Aeronautics in 1944 and adapted techniques which he had used for fuselage shell structures. Hoff's work was, in turn, based on the "relaxation" method developed by Prof R. V. Southwell at Oxford prewar and developed during the war.

'Hoff had applied these methods to rectangular sheet structures, but we applied them to structures of more general shapes. The methods which we developed for the Lightning have evolved into the finite element method which is in general application today. The use of the computer proved that our previous "hand" method, although terribly slow, was basically

correct. As a result of this work we produced a wing which was multi-spar and multi-rib, a fairly complicated structure, and one which needed a great deal of localised reinforcement in the rear half of the inboard wing and the centre section. In structural tests which were carried out, the strain gauges showed that our analysis was quite good. We did find, however, that the internal structure of the centre wing was grossly overstressed in the original design and we reduced the stresses by removing material to make selected members lighter and more flexible. As well as calculating stresses, we had to find out how a wing with such a large sweepback would twist, camber and generally distort. We were up against problems of aileron reversal which had shown themselves in other aircraft at that time, loss of lift and the dynamic instability known as flutter. In addition we had the problem of integrating fuel into this unusual wing.

'When it came to the fuselage, the main problem was installing the engines. Very few aircraft of that time had engines inside the fuselage, and it was difficult to calculate the heating effects which this would produce. Quite a lot of the structure had to be designed for high temperatures. This meant the use of titanium, and the Lightning was probably the first aircraft in Europe to use this metal. It constituted around five per cent of the fuselage structure weight. It was used in the structure between the engines and in the rear fuselage. Because of engine-heating and kinetic heating resulting from the aircraft's supersonic

performance, components were subject to wide ranges of temperature, and we had to find out how material strengths changed over a long time.

'Once again, new techniques were evolved to handle a problem which, in previous aircraft, had been ignored. The all-moving tailplane also involved some novel structural ideas. In the past, tailplanes had been mounted on beams which passed right through the fuselage and were easy to mount, but those on the Lightning were mounted separately on pivots which were subject to enormous loads. As in the case of the wing, the structure and its actuating mechanism were also designed to avoid problems from distortion and flutter. The ACE computer was used in the analysis and solution of the flutter problem: the second area in which we pioneered the use of modern computing techniques in the UK.'

Below left: With the ground and buildings just a blur, P1A shows its very fast paces in one of the early flights out of Warton. / *BAe*

Right: The 'stalking horse' for the Lightning, the SB5. The SB5 had interchangeable wings and tail. In this picture it has a high tail and a 50° sweep. / *Shorts*

Below: The SB5 configured with the tail in the high position and with a wing sweep of 60°. / *Shorts*

Model Lightnings

Mr I. R. Yates, an engineer and a specialist in flutter work said that three $\frac{1}{7}$-scale models were made at Warton each based on two rockets produced by the English Electric guided weapons company to test the 60° sweep wings. The rockets were fired at the army ranges at Larkhill to show whether such a design would be subject to flutter because there was a dearth of theoretical information:

'We used the ACE computer to work out the way in which the aircraft would vibrate. We were at the sharp end of research. Rudder buzz developed on flight 13 of the P1B in the transonic phase. The cure was to remove a section of the top of the rudder. We were working with crude wind tunnel models and mechanical desk calculators. One had to think fundamentally why the results which we produced were like that. Nowadays the computer is becoming a substitute for thinking'

Mr B. O. Heath worked as a stressman on the project, he said that the problem of the day (1948) was that the aeroplane had to go supersonic without reheat. Reheat was regarded as something that might be unreliable and which might not even work. In the event it did and the aeroplane, designed to go supersonic without it, was really 'hot' with it. Its initial design diving speed was exceeded in a climb.

'We did not know enough about side intakes then so we decided we would have a front intake. There was a great debate as to what the wing shape should be, in which the delta was a strong contender. We found that the majority of the lift in a delta was towards its front so we "did away with" the rear part of the wing (which contributed drag) and applied it more usefully as a low-set tailplane. There was also a great debate with the Royal Aircraft Establishment about what the wing should be. They thought that 60° was too much of a risk and that we should fly with 50° first and then 60°. They also wanted to use a very high-set tailplane. The outcome of this controversy was the SB5 experimental aircraft. This proved to be misleading even when fitted with its wing of high sweep. All that it was to show was that a notch in the leading edge of the wing was a good idea.

'To help us in our aerodynamic loading work we took every report that had been found in Germany at the end of the war, including work on the V2 and other wartime aircraft and missiles — some of the papers were stamped with the German wartime eagle — and from the United States. The Americans produced a lot of test reports, some of which they neglected to use themselves, but which they had no objection to other western nations using.

'Because it flew so fast, the Lightning (P1) was the first time account had to be taken of structural distortion from the start of design. Rocket models were fired to check flutter (vibration) calculations. The Warton team at the time was very young, mostly in their 20s, but were working in an area where there was little experience anyway. By a great deal of personal application and the use of what was available, sound judgements were made and a safe and powerful weapon emerged as a result. Some 400-500 people were working on the project in the early days. Who was responsible for the Lightning? Many of the concepts were those of the late Ray Creasey, who was a brilliant aerodynamicist. Petter was the leader of the design team but F. W. Page took over when Petter went to Follands.

'Another quantum jump with the Lightning was the introduction of power controls which English Electric had tested in a Halifax. Other problems were to design an undercarriage to retract into a very thin wing, and later to stop canopies flying off. We lost a number, and one which lifted off at Mach 1.5 at approximately 25,000ft flew down to earth (like a modern lifting-body research aircraft) landing on a compost heap. The only damage to it was scratches where the owner had dragged it into a potting shed. We closely examined the cams which held the canopy in place and modified them and the actuating mechanism so that they were no longer actuated by "hair-trigger" action.'

Edward Loveless was assistant chief stressman to F. W. Page, and later chief stressman. He worked on the stress calculations on the Lightning project and later saw most of them proved correct on the test rigs which were set up in the mechanical laboratories at Warton.

There was, he said, an error in the estimate of the stability and strength of the structure in two places, namely the upper wing skin just forward of the rear spar at the fuselage side and also in the rear fuselage itself. In each case the skin was buckling under the rig loads before ultimate loading was reached. This came as a surprise to the designers who had increased the thickness of the wing skin in the above area to $\frac{3}{4}$in to carry the correctly assessed loading but felt that such a thickness would not buckle without causing a sudden collapse of the structure. The problems were solved in

Above: Nearly completed Lightnings at Samlesbury. After roll-out at Samblesbury, each new machine was flown to the company airfield at Warton for test flying. / *BAe*

Right: The familiar shape of the Lightning wing is easily identifiable on one of the ⅐th scale models which were made at Warton and Preston to test the 60° sweepback. The test wings were flown on rocket motors produced by the English Electric guided weapons division at speeds up to Mach 1.85. The first two were clamped between twin 5in rockets, but the third model was a cleaner vehicle powered by a single rocket motor of a larger diameter. The models were fired at the army ranges at Larkhill in 1954 to show whether such a design would be subject to flutter, as there was a dearth of theoretical information. The telemetry traces showed that although the wing did vibrate, it was damped and there was no flutter or divergence.

a fairly straightforward manner by introducing additional stiffeners.

One other problem which showed itself on initial undercarriage testing on the aircraft was that on lowering the undercarriage it would not completely lower but stopped some 11° short of the 'down' position. Designed and successfully rig-tested by British Messier, once again there was a fairly simple solution. Attachment lugs were cut off and an extra bracket introduced to give the extra leverage which was required to overcome the friction which was building up, the degree of which had been slightly underestimated by the designers.

Trevor Williams was the production manager for the project. He recalled that production started with the 'hand-crafting' of five prototypes, followed by a run of 20 pre-production aircraft before the main production phase began. Some interesting new techniques were developed by English Electric in building the Lightning, techniques which were completely different from those which had been used on earlier aircraft. In these they had built the structure and then put the fuel tank inside, whereas on the Lightning the wing was the fuel tank, and this created problems in attaining fuel 'tightness'. To ensure that the riveting was so tight that there was no possibility of a fuel leak, EE developed a special form of countersunk rivet in which a ridge within the countersink bit into the rivet head to form a seal.

Welding was introduced into the primary structure to an extent that had not previously been used in airframe construction in Britain, including into the tailplane bearing, where it was very effective and very much cheaper than trying to machine the part out of a block of metal. This was a development from the industrial techniques of general engineering and was a reversal of the usual trend for aerospace developments to be passed on to general engineering. At the same time, many conventional techniques were employed in production. A lot of bolts and rivets were used for parts of the aircraft which, today, would be machined from the solid.

EE had a great fund of engineering expertise. The factory at Preston had never made aeroplanes out of 'stick and string', but had entered the business just before World War II (although there had been an earlier period from 1914 to 1925 when they made flying boats) to make other people's designs under licence. From Victorian times, the Strand Road works in Preston had produced a range of commercial engineering products, including railway rolling stock, diesel engines, tramcars and trolley buses. When they moved into aeroplanes, they tackled them in a different way to that of the traditional aircraft industry, and

that attitude had had a profound effect on EE's 'own' aeroplanes, the Canberra and the Lightning. Producing the Lightning was a tremendous challenge as it was such a great leap forward from the Canberra and taxed the engineering ingenuity of everybody in the company.

There was no doubt that technology learned in the Lightning went into the later Jaguar and multi-role Tornado. The Strand Road factory tooled up to produce six Lightnings a month, but during the whole production period, which ran from 1960 until 1968

Below left: Lightnings coming down the assembly line in 1961 — it was the first picture to be released of Britain's 'top-secret' fighter. At the peak, production rose to four aircraft a month. / *BAe*

Right: Largely to make access easier, the nose section of each Lightning was made in two sections split lengthways from front to back. Here the halves in their separate jigs in the Preston factory are shortly to be united. / *BAe*

Below: Lightning nose sections are completed at the English Electric works at Strand Road in the centre of Preston where railway wagons and tramcars were produced in an earlier era. / *BAe*

(although spares and replacement parts for Lightnings in service were produced for more than a decade after that) the rate did not go higher than four a month. The aircraft was built up in a small number of large sections. There was the front fuselage, which was made in two halves. This was also the air intake for the engines, with the cockpit on top, and the main reason for the decision to split it into two was to provide better access for the workers on the production line.

Then there was the main fuselage, the wings and undercarriage, and the moving tail. Major frames in the fuselage which supported large loads were machined integrally, while some other components, such as the canopy frame, were forged. Titanium was introduced — probably for the first time in aircraft construction in Britain. It was used in sheet form in the engine bay because the high temperatures found there would have been too much for the more traditional aerospace metals. Strand Road developed the welding of titanium and the forming of sheets of the metal under heat, and although a certain amount of 'know-how' was obtained from the United States, EE used their own expertise so that by the time the Lightning was in production they were as advanced in the use of titanium as any country in the world.

Tony Simmons was the English Electric electronic systems specialist who developed the requirements for the weapons system which was eventually to go into the Lightning. He based his work on a series of calculations which began during the years 1950-51. This work showed that to have any chance of manoeuvring and aiming at an enemy aircraft it was necessary to know exactly where that aircraft was when the attacking aircraft was up to 20 miles away and flying at a high supersonic speed. This meant that there would have to be a radar on the front end of the Lightning with a range of up to 20 miles, capable of searching, finding and locking on.

This was quite a tall order, considering that existing radars at that time had a range of some five miles, while people had no real idea of how to set one aircraft on to another. The Firestreak air-to-air guided missile was being developed at that time. It had a lead sulphide cell capable of seeing heated bodies such as the inside of an aircraft's jet pipe, but that meant that you had to get your fighter around to the back of the bomber. This restricted the speed of the fighter in its turn on to the rear of the bomber to Mach 1.3 and it could obviously not make full use of the top speed of the Lightning, planned to be in excess of Mach 2. With Firestreak it was, therefore impossible to catch a supersonic bomber travelling at high speeds and so the Lightning Weapon System was further developed to use Red Top, a missile equipped with an infra-red cell capable not only of seeing heated bodies, but also heated carbon dioxide. This meant that the pilot of the intercepting aircraft could approach his target from an angle of something like 45° off dead ahead and rely on his air-to-air missiles homing on to the efflux of the jet engines. For this battle technique you also had to have an improved radar, and an improved method of laying it off on to the target.

In the event, the Marks 1 and 2 Lightnings were equipped with Firestreak, developed by de Havilland Propellers, at Hatfield, and the Ferranti AI23 radar, developed at Edinburgh, while the Marks 3, 5, 6, 53 and 55 had Red Top and the much improved AI23B radar. Having decided on the parameters for the radar, the basic question arose of where, in the tightly-packed fuselage, to stow it. Fortunately at about the same time the need for a centre-body 'bullet' in the air intake to the engines became apparent if the air was to reach the engines at maximum efficiency so that the Lightning could progress beyond about Mach 1.6 to Mach 2 and more. The decision was made to put the radar inside this centre body.

How does the AI23 radar work? Basically, it locks on to the target and then instructs the pilot in which direction to fly the aircraft to keep the target in sight. Meanwhile the homing eyes of the missiles have been slaved to look in the same direction as the radar. Eventually they signal that they have seen the target. The pilot receives a signal that he is in range, presses the 'commit' button and the missiles decide when to fire. Ranges at which the missiles operate are still on the secret list, but the author's speculation is that they fire when the target is around three miles distant. At one stage in the development of the Lightning weapons system it was decided to go for Auto-Attack, in which the autopilot would have linked the radar to the aircraft controls and so steered itself on the target. A prototype system was actually fitted to an aircraft and flown successfully but this expensive addition was abandoned in 1956 along with the TSR2 and many other major and minor defence projects.

Frank Roe and Ron Dickson were employed respectively on wind-tunnel research and aerodynamic research at the time of the project. They recalled how in the middle of 1948 they, as very young employees of English Electric, earning something around £7 a week, were called to join the small team which was to initiate the P1A (which led to the Lightning), a team which had as its main members F. W. Page, Dai Ellis, a first-class mechanical engineer, and Ray Creasey, who they considered to be responsible for the design concept of the Lightning, all reporting to W. E. W. Petter, as chief engineer. There was a fairly big debate at the time over two things, the decision to go to a thin 60° wing sweep, and a fuselage with as small a frontal area as possible to minimise wave drag, both of which they considered necessary to give supersonic performance without re-heat, which at that time was in its infancy. Considerations of longitudinal distribution of cross section area led to the centre fuselage having a constant section and flat sides. They were unable to produce an even thinner wing, because of the structural limitations of the time, and the need to accommodate the undercarriage, even though the wheels were designed to be extremely thin, with high-pressure tyres.

The early design had conventional streamwise wing tips but they soon found from wind-tunnel tests that on wings with such a sweepback the ailerons would have been ineffective. In 1953 when they were looking at possible developments of the aircraft they considered putting on a delta wing. But wind-tunnel tests showed that this would have de-stabilised the aircraft. When they started to design the Lightning the wing was low down so that the engines were 'staggered' with the top one farther forward than the bottom one. The tail also started off high in the designs, but they quickly found that with a low wing and a high tail the wing leading-edge vortices caused pitch-up so that the conclusion was reached that with a 60° sweep the tailplane had to be below the wing plane. The tail was therefore lowered, and in order to raise the wing the stagger of the engines was reversed to today's configuration in which the lower engine is to the fore. They warned RAE that they were going to have trouble with their designs for the SB5 research aircraft with a high tail, and this also proved to be the case through a long range of aircraft, including the Javelin fighter, and the early BAC 1-11 and Boeing 727 airliners, all of which suffered deep-stall symptoms.

Roe and Dickson recalled that the supersonic wind tunnel which was built for the Lightning, using a Nene with 5,000lb thrust, and with a slotted, working section, was the first of its kind in Europe. It was able to simulate speeds of up to Mach 1.07, and part of it now rests in the Science Museum, London.

Len Milsom joined the Lightning team in 1957 as a mechanical engineer and was at once involved in problems of engine and airframe heating. At the speeds at which the Lightning was designed to fly the heating on the skin would be 75°C at low altitude in Britain and in tropical climates 100°C at low level and 120°C at altitude. The structure used a lot of simple aluminium alloys which deteriorated at high temperatures, and the worry was over what degree of thermal fatigue this was going to produce. The engine was a, 'pretty hot beast', producing outside temperatures in the order of 300°C. In an effort to keep down the degree of heat reaching the aircraft systems, which because of the slim design of the Lightning, were packed into a confined space, and the airframe, the jet pipes were painted with a special paint containing a certain amount of gold, the cost of which was £75 a pound — a great deal of money indeed in those days.

Other methods found to cool the airframe and systems from engine heat included lagging and ventilation, while to prevent kinetic fatigue, some vulnerable parts were changed to steel titanium from aluminium . A further worry was the effect of high-speed flight on the cockpit windscreen where the temperature gradient would be high; the outside would be heated up to high temperatures while the inside would be cooled by the air conditioning. Hot gas leaking from the joints between the engines and the intermediate pipes between the engines and the re-heat units heated the aircraft structure and caused fires. These leaks had to be plugged, and more titanium was put in in crucial areas. Fuel and hydraulic lines passing close to the engines had to be re-routed. These were all piecemeal attacks on the problem with the idea of trying not to spend too much money. Keeping the pilot cool also presented a series of problems which had to be solved, and these problems recurred when the aircraft was sent abroad to carry out tropical trials.

Below: Component parts were taken by road to the works at Samlesbury, Lancashire, where final assembly took place. Here a rear and a front fuselage are about to be mated. / *BAe*

Champagne Christening

The Lightning was given its name on 23 October 1958, when in a ceremony at RAE, Farnborough, it was christened by having a bottle of champagne broken over its nose by the then Chief of the Air Staff, Sir Dermot Boyle. A note on the occasion issued at the time by English Electric recalled that it had been officially stated that the Lightning would probably be the last conventional jet fighter for the RAF, as the 1957 Defence White Paper had stated that the Service was unlikely to require any more advanced fighters. 'The company considers that the Lightning will continue to be developed and operated for 10 years', EE commented — a somewhat pessimistic comment, in view of the fact that the aircraft continued to be operated by RAF squadrons, and in Saudi Arabia, in the 1980s.

On that day in 1958, the company recorded that both single-seat and two-seat Lightnings were in large-scale production at their works at Preston and Samlesbury, and that the advanced test programme was proceeding. The Lightning had been flown by more than 30 different pilots, including those from RAE, the Aeroplane and Armament Experimental Establishment, at Boscombe Down, and the Central Fighter Establishment. Evaluations by these pilots had, 'ensured that the Service is kept fully informed of the progress with the aircraft and its advanced weapon system.' A Royal Air Force pilot, Sqn Ldr J. Dell, was permanently attached to the company's flight operations department, and under the direction of Mr R. P. Beamont, the company's chief test pilot, was taking part in the actual test flying. Beamont had completed more than 300 test missions at that date, Dell over 50. Overall responsibility for the design and development of the Lightning rested with F. W. Page, chief engineer of the company's aircraft division, EE recorded.

These were great days for English Electric, and the company proudly recalled that the naming ceremony was the second to be carried out within seven years. On 19 January 1951, the then Prime Minister of Australia, Mr R. G. Menzies, had formally named the first British jet bomber the Canberra and at a ceremony at Biggin Hill airfield had broken a bottle of

Australian champagne over the nose of that aircraft. Since then, 1,200 Canberras had been built, including nearly 400 under licence in the United States and others in Australia, and the type was in service with nine air forces throughout the world. Hopes were obviously high at that time of a sale of Lightnings to the United States, for the point was made at the Lightning naming ceremony that an aircraft had been flown by an official evaluation team, and that they had paid, 'enthusiastic tribute' to its qualities, and in particular to its outstanding climb and acceleration. Sir Dermot Boyle made the announcement, and Sir George Nelson, chairman of English Electric, added that the Americans had taken back with them what he described as, 'the most glowing accounts' of the Lightning.

The evaluation had been carried out by two pilots, Lt-Col Anderson, chief of the flight test operations division of Edwards air force base, California, and Capt D. K. Slayton, of the operations division of the same base. With them to England came a senior technical adviser, Mr Ken Lush, who had gone to the US in 1951 after previous employment at the AAEE, Boscombe Down. During their trials, which were carried out from the EE airfield at Warton, the two Americans flew the Lightning to the performance limits which were specified for it in service. They were briefed on it by Mr Beamont, who a short while before their visit had been in the United States flying several of the USAF Century series fighters. The American aviators duly returned home. Nothing more was heard of any US desire to take the Lightning into service, and the evaluation was eventually attributed on the British side to nothing more than the polite exchane of cockpits which usually goes on between friendly air forces when they have something new to show off.

Information to the public about the progress of the Lightning project was, in the early days, extremely sparse, and what announcements there were showed obvious signs of being heavily filtered through the government security sieve. The majority of the announcements were inevitably 'bullish', but signs of one area of trouble were there for anybody with more than a superficial interest in aviation to see when, on 2 September 1955, English Electric said abruptly that it was unlikely that the P1 would appear at the first day of the Farnborough show following the loss of its cockpit canopy in flight. First flight of the P1B, from Warton on 4 April 1957, was the occasion for some drum beating. The P1B, it was explained by EE, had been designed from the outset as a complete weapons system, with its extensive armament, radar and radio

Right: The christening of the Lightning for the RAF at Farnborough in October 1958. / *The Times*

aids as integral parts of the aircraft, and not treated a extra items to be added in stages.

This equipment — long-range radar to find enemy aircraft by day and night and in all weathers, radio and navigation aids for operations under the worst conditions, and a dual armament of guided missiles and 30mm Aden cannon — was of equal importance to the aircraft's supersonic speed. Although externally similar to the P1A research aeroplanes, the P1B had a redesigned fuselage to accommodate its much more powerful engines, and the large volume of radio, radar and armament equipment. The cockpit was refrigerated, and air below freezing was pumped into it, as well as to much of the equipment in the aircraft, in order to overcome the effects of kinetic heating (the so-called thermal barrier) at high speeds. The refrigeration unit produced 150 times as much cooling air as an average domestic refrigerator. Three P1B prototypes would be followed by another 20 fully-equipped pre-production aircraft, each of which would be used for the further development of a particular facet of supersonic fighter interception, such as the navigation aids, radio, armament, automatic pilot, engines, radar, handling and operational trials.

In this way, the clearance for the RAF of this advanced and complex weapon system would be achieved more quickly than if only three or four prototypes were available, as was the case with earlier British military aircraft. Among equipment supplied by other members of the English Electric group of companies which would be carried in the P1B was Marconi radio, and an electrical supply system, actuators and electric motors designed and manufactured by the company's aircraft equipment division. Because of the complexity of the P1B, EE were putting a very considerable effort into speeding the long test programme, but this would inevitably take many months to complete. The close liasion between the company and the Ministry of Supply which had been maintained since the start of the P1 design would continue, and they would both provide a number of test pilots at various stages in the programme.

Further company drum beating followed in mid-July, 1957, when a P1, flown by Beamont, beat the existing world speed record. The company was unable, it said, for security reasons to state the precise speed which had been reached, but it did point out coyly that the world speed record stood at 1,132mph, held by the Fairey Delta FD2. No attempt had been made by the P1 to capture this record. When the aircraft reached a speed in excess of this record it was still accelerating, and the pilot throttled back. EE told the public that the P1B was powered by Rolls-Royce Avon turbojets, but that the P1A, which by that time had completed three years of research flying, had Armstrong Siddeley Sapphire turbojets.

Justifying the P1's twin-engine design, the company said that this design had several major advantages. It could be flown on one engine, so making it easy for a pilot to return to base if one engine failed. Because of their design, glide approaches by supersonic aircraft were extremely hazardous, thus an engine failure in a single-engined supersonic aircraft generally resulted in the pilot baling out and the aircraft being lost. With two engines, the P1 could maintain supersonic speed without using reheat. This meant that less fuel was used than would be the case if one engine with a large amount of reheat was fitted. The two engines also allowed a complete and thorough duplication of all the essential services to the aircraft. If one engine failed, the aircraft did not develop asymmetric characteristics, because both engines exhausted along the centreline of the fuselage. By setting one engine in front of, and rather below, the other, the aircraft had the thrust of two engines for the frontal area of appreciably less than two.

Autostabilisation was fitted to the P1B to make the task of flying the aircraft as simple as possible. This would give the pilot time to concentrate on the actual interception of the target while the aircraft flew itself. This meant that no second crew member was needed. But autostabilisation was not an essential safety device, because the P1 and the P1B were inherently stable and easy to fly. This was proved by the fact that pilots who had made only three flights in other swept-wing aircraft had flown the P1 with complete success. The tailplane had been placed low down in relation to the fin. This avoided the characteristic pitch-up movement which occurred in aircraft designed for high speeds when they were flying subsonically and transonically if the tailplane was high on the fin. The P1 had no pitch-up or other aerodynamic vices.

The aircraft was large enough to accommodate the more sophisticated guided missiles which would be developed in the next few years, and their associated equipment. Special instruments had been developed for the P1. These included a roller-blind attitude

indicator which replaced the artificial horizon, and which was not subject to 'topple' at high angles of climb, so enabling the pilot to make steep and accurate turns.

Comprehensive ground testing of the P1 and its components had been carried out. This had included hundreds of hours 'flying' in both low and high-speed wind tunnels at Warton, and the stressing to destruction of a complete air-frame. In addition, the prototype aircraft had completed more than 600 proving flights covering handling, performance, stability and gun firing. Details of a test flight by the P1B were issued in February 1958. The flight was from Boscombe Down and lasted 30 minutes, 23 minutes of which were flown continuously at supersonic speed, the EE announcement said. The aircraft reached supersonic speed one minute after take-off and arrived overhead at Warton aerodrome 19 minutes later. The distance covered was approximately 180 nautical miles. At the controls was R. P. Beamont. When it reached Warton, the aircraft remained airborne and carried out a series of high-speed tests, using reheat. 'This sustained supersonic performance emphasises the faster - than - sound capabilities of the P1B'.

Through such snippets, the progress of the

Below left: Overwing tanks on test on a Mark 2 prototype in 1961. The tank tail fins were later dispensed with. The tanks were designed for ferrying and on the F6 increased the non-stop range by 250nm to 1,350nm. The tanks each had a capacity of 2,160lb of fuel. The fuel could be dumped and the tanks jettisoned if the Lightning was involved in combat. / *BAe via R. P. Beamont*

Below: Dear old pals. A Lightning two-seat keeps company on the apron with a Hurricane and a Spitfire, representative of an RAF era a little earlier and a lot slower. / *The Times*

Top right: With the remains of the christening bottle of champagne visible in the rear, the Lightning for the RAF was named in a ceremony at RAE Farnborough on 23 October 1958 by the Chief of the Air Staff Sir Dermot Boyle, in the company of the chairman of English Electric, Sir George Nelson. / *The Times*

Centre right: All polished up for the Paris air salon of 1963 was this prototype T5 XM966 (converted from a T4), Red Top at the ready. / *Brian M. Service*

Below right: Something of an historic RAF moment at the 1962 Farnborough show as No 92 Squadron Hunter F6s are led in formation by the aircraft which were to replace them in the Service, Lightning F1s. / *Brian M. Service*

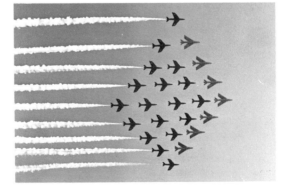

Lightning was charted for the general public, but so tight was the security net that very few details of any worth were getting out. Against this background, the news that experiments were to take place in fitting a rocket-boost engine to the Lightning, given in February 1958, was remarkably forthcoming — ironically so, in view of the fact, recorded earlier in this book, that the experiments were later discontinued. The rocket would be a Napier Double-Scorpion, English Electric were allowed to say, and several aircraft would take part in the trials which were to be carried out under a contract with the Ministry of Supply. The rocket engine was intended as an optional power plant so that the P1B could be operated as either a mixed-power plant or pure-jet fighter, depending entirely on the type of operation undertaken.

With the rocket, the P1B would be able to fly at very high altitudes where the atmosphere was thin and the power of jet engines was consequently considerably reduced, and to make exceptionally rapid climbs to intercept enemy bombers when the warning period was extremely short. It was made clear that the Lightning would retain its two Rolls-Royce Avon turbojets when fitted with the rocket engine, and it was pointed out that: 'for most operations these turbojets provide ample power and superior endurance. But in certain limited operations the introduction of a proportion of rocket power is advantageous.'

A special rocket motors pack had been designed for the aircraft. It was fitted to the underside of the fuselage. Besides housing the motor, the pack also contained the high-test peroxide oxidant for the rocket, and the whole assembly was jettisonable. The high-test peroxide was used in conjunction with kerosene drawn from the aircraft's normal fuel tanks. The rocket engine pack had been specifically designed to make handling and refuelling with high-test peroxide a safe and straightforward matter, either with the pack in place on the aircraft, or detached from it. The Double-Scorpion rocket engine was designed and developed at Luton by D. Napier and Son Ltd, which was part of the English Electric aviation group.

Close liasion had been maintained between Napier and the aircraft division of EE in the work, which had included extensive flight testing of the rocket engine in a Canberra. In August 1957, it was revealed that a Canberra fitted with a Double-Scorpion had set a new official world altitude record. The Double-Scorpion was a relatively small motor, measuring 33.75in long by 23in wide, but it had a particularly high thrust — although security prevented publication of the actual power. The twin barrels could be fired together or separately, depending on the thrust required. The

Above left: A gendarme keeps an eye on T5 XM966 at the 1963 Paris air show. / *Brian M. Service*

Above: No 111 Squadron from Wattisham showed this F3 XR716 at the 1965 Paris air show. Much in evidence is the badge of the Squadron (motto: *Standing By*). This is the Jerusalem Cross, which commemorates the fact that the squadron was formed in Palestine on 1 August 1917. On the cross are imposed three scimitars. The lightning flash can be seen passing through the RAF roundel on the nose. No 111 were first issued with the F1A in the spring of 1961, but re-equipped with the Mark 3 from the end of 1964, forming an aerobatics team the following year. / *Brian M. Service*

rocket operated when the pilot pressed a button in the cockpit. Rapid starting was achieved using the thermal principle with a catalyst, and the engine could be stopped and started at any altitude.

Breakthrough of the Lightning to twice the speed of sound was announced publicly on 6 January 1959, when it was also stated that the aircraft was capable of flying, 'at even higher speeds'. Mach 2 was reached during level flight at high altitude, and was maintained with the use of minimum reheat. 'This performance makes the Lightning the fastest twin-engined, all-weather fighter in full production in the world', English Electric said. Once again the pilot was R. P. Beamont, who reported after attaining Mach 2 that although that particular aircraft was not fitted with auto-

stabilisation, the control and stability were eminently satisfactory.

High speed runs leading up to Mach 2 had been started ten miles north of Colwyn Bay, where the aircraft were accelerated from Mach .95 at 35,000ft by using reheat on the Avons. The flights were northwards towards the Wigtownshire coast and were under radar control to reduce the effects of supersonic bangs over the land.

A simple conversion of the basic Lightning was the two-seat trainer, the first flight of which took place in May 1959, a fortnight ahead of schedule, the company claimed. With Beamont at the controls, it went supersonic 15 minutes after take-off and was airborne for a total of 30 minutes. Afterwards, Bee commented, 'It handled just as well as the single-seater Lightning, and perhaps even better.' English Electric said that the first flight would ensure that trainers would be available for pilot conversion at an early stage in the operational life of the Lightning with the RAF. The trainer had side-by-side seating for instructor and pupil, and its performance was comparable to that of the single-seater version. Two-seaters were already in production in parallel with the single-seater version.

One of the first top people to try out the two-seater was the commander-in-chief of Fighter Command, ACM Sir Thomas Pike who flew at speeds of up to

1,121mph on 7 July 1959. He was accompanied by Bee, but Sir Thomas flew the aircraft for most of the 33 minutes they were airborne, making a rapid climb to 40,000ft, and then accelerating to nearly twice the speed of sound. Although the first Lightnings had gone to the Central Fighter Establishment at Coltishall in December 1959, the first operational unit, also at Coltishall, did not receive them until July 1960, and the Farnborough show of that autumn provided a fine arena in which to show off the RAF's new 'toy'.

Bee and Jimmy Dell flew the two aircraft. Some important new claims were made for the Lightning at that time. It had shown, they said, the effectiveness of its combination of 30mm cannon and two Firestreak homing missiles, or 48 two-inch spin-stabilised ROE rockets in Microcell launchers, and how unerringly its Ferranti Airpass radar led it to its target. Its performance could match the threat of any modern bomber, while retaining sufficient flexibility in the design to make use of later weapons. This was leading to the development of new and most promising marks of the Lightning. 'The Lightning is not a single small step forward from the subsonic jet fighter', EE claimed. 'It has more than twice the performance of these aircraft, and brings with it a host of new techniques and systems which make it by far the most effective fighter any air force in the free world has ever possessed.'

Precise performance figures remained secret at that time, but it could be stated that it had an, 'astonishingly' high rate of climb, which brought it to the altitude of the highest-flying bomber a very few minutes after being ordered into the air. It had the endurance to complete very difficult interceptions. The Lightning could also be flown from one side of the world to the other with the help of midair refuelling. And in a reference to the previous controversy with RAE over the basic design of the Lightning, the company went on:
'The tailplane is low down in relation to the fin. This avoids the characteristic pitch-up movement which occurs in aircraft designed for high speeds when they are flying subsonically and transonically if the tailplane is high on the fin. The Lightning has no pitch-up or any other aerodynamic vices. It is large enough to accommodate the more advanced guided missiles which are now being developed, and their associated equipment.'

By December 1960, with the first RAF squadrons working up, English Electric were allowed to give, for the first time, the top speed of the Lightning — 1,500mph. Precise performance figures were still secret, but during routine operations aircraft had been flying at speeds well in excess of 1,200mph. Top speed was of equal importance to its equipment which enabled it to find its target and to fire its missiles or guns to, 'complete the kill'. Three armament combinations could be carried by the Lightning — two Firestreak air-to-air homing missiles and two 30mm cannon; two batteries of 24 two-inch air-to-air rockets and two 30mm cannon; or four 30mm cannon.

English Electric, at the same time, once again set the stage for their hoped-for developments of the aircraft,

pointing out that performance and 'stretch' capability were such as to make the best possible use of current weapons, and to take advantage of future ones. 'It is this basic design philosophy which is making the new versions possible', the company claimed. By 1963 the first of the 'stretched' versions had appeared, the Mark 3, to the accompaniment of stories in the newspapers that its performance was so good that it was able to intercept the high-flying American U2 reconnaissance aircraft. The interceptions were with the agreement of the United States Air Force and took place around nine miles high, the Lightnings appearing, according to contemporary reports, 'to sit effortlessly on the U2's wingtips'.

Derek Wood, *Sunday Telegraph* Air Correspondent, wrote on 26 May 1963, that to provide the necessary control facilities to enable the Lightning Mark 3 to intercept and destroy very high-flying aircraft in all weathers, the RAF had ordered a computer system, made by Elliott, known as Fire Brigade. This would accept radar information on the enemy, work out the optimum flight path to the target, and the return to a suitable base. With Fire Brigade

and the Lightning 3, the ground controller would be able to send the aircraft automatically to its target. When the Lightning had been put within range of the target, the weapons system on the aircraft would take over, fire either rocket projectiles or Red Top guided missiles.

The news that RAF squadrons were being re-equipped with the Mark 3 only four years after receiving their original Lightnings was not officially released until 1964 when the British Aircraft Corporation, which had by that time swallowed English Electric, claimed that the Mark 3 was so advanced in aircraft and equipment performance that it constituted virtually a new interceptor weapons system, superior to any other in the world. Compared with earlier marks, the 3 had more powerful engines, improved performance, and more advanced radar, navigation and fire-control equipment. It could attack with collision-course weapons which were radar-guided and computer-launched at optimum point to cope with closing speeds approaching 3,000mph. The latest stage in the development of the Mark 3 had been the introduction of a cambered leading edge wing and

a new, larger, ventral fuel tank which strikingly improved the performance and operational flexibility of the aircraft. The outer portion of the leading edge of the wing had been extended to incorporate camber in the developed Mark 3. These developments had been tried in a series of test flights by Bee in the P1. The developed Mark 3 made its maiden flight from the BAC works at Fllton, Bristol, on 17 April 1964.

These changes materially reduced subsonic drag and significantly improved cruising range. Take-off and landing characteristics were also slightly improved. The improved range resulting from the cambered wing was further extended by the greatly increased capacity of the new ventral tank. The extra

Below left: No 11 Squadron Lightnings at the ready. No 11 became the third squadron to equip with F6s, taking them on to the inventory at Leuchars in April 1967. / *MoD via A. Price*

Below: Pilots of No 56 Squadron at Akrotiri, Cyprus, dash to their aircraft for a practice scramble. / *MoD via A. Price*

fuel which this carried provided extended patrol time, greater reheat acceleration capacity, and longer supersonic endurance for use during interception and attack, plus the ability to recover to a desired base from a greater distance. BAC explained that the advantages of the cambered wing were first investigated and test flown with the first prototype P1 but the subsonic gain was not at that time a necessary adjunct to the Lightning's performance in its role as an interceptor fighter in the United Kingdom's sophisticated defence system.

The tactical requirement had, however, broadened with subsequent trends in world events and with the demonstration of the ability to deploy Lightnings rapidly to overseas theatres, through the development of flight refuelling, and the provision of overwing tanks. To maintain directional stability at high supersonic speeds, the new fuel tank had two additional ventral fins aft. The new wing contour resulted in plain, unbalanced ailerons, completely inset, but there was no change in span, and no effect on lateral control or stability. 'Dizzy' de Villiers, chief production test pilot of BAC's Preston division, flew

the first long-range Mark 3 to come off the production line on 16 June 1965. The flight was from Samlesbury airfield and was de Villiers' 1,000th Lightning test flight. BAC recorded at the time that he was the third member of the Warton test pilot team to reach this target, both Bee and Jimmy Dell having got the '1,000 up' by then, although Bee was first in the field by many months.

Nearly 8,000 Lightning test flights had been made by the summer of 1965, and over 5,000 of these had been at supersonic speeds. Mark 5 trainer versions of the Lightning were cleared for issue to the RAF from BAC on 29 March 1965, and the final proving flight in the production test schedule was carried out jointly from Warton by de Villiers and Sqn Ldr R. L. Davis, officer commanding No 226 Operational Conversion Unit, RAF Coltishall. It was the first time that the clearance flight of the first production aircraft of a new mark had been performed 'dual' by a pilot from both the manufacturer and the customer.

The second production Mark 5 was delivered from Warton to Boscombe Down on the following day, flown by Dell accompanied by P. J. Moneypenny, chief navigator of the Preston division. News that the developed Mark 3 Lightning was to be designated the

Mark 6 by the Ministry of Aviation was released to the public by BAC on 25 April 1966. By that time, the company said, the Mark 6 had successfully completed flight refuelling trials over the Irish Sea at maximum all-up weight, carrying twin overwing ferrying tanks and a flight refuelling probe. In this configuration, the aerodynamics had proved better than was anticipated and the handling qualities of the aircraft remained exceptionally good, being free from buffet or trim change in the subsonic region.

Compared with earlier marks, the Lightnings Mark

Below: Ground crew work on No 56 Squadron Lightnings at Akrotiri, Cyprus. They are about to clip on a Firestreak missile, while another Firestreak, a protective 'Noddy cap' cover over its nose, stands on its dolly in the foreground. / *MoD via A. Price*

Right: Using a special crane, RAF mechanics lift out the centre body from the air intake for the twin Avon engines. The centre body directs the flow of air at supersonic speed and also contains the radar. / *MoD via A. Price*

Below right: As this picture of the exposed upper Avon indicates, there is no room to spare in the Lightning engine bays. Leaking fuel pipes produced problems, including several engine fires, in the early days. / *MoD via A. Price*

41

3, 5 and 6, and the Marks 53 and 55 which were by that time in production for the Royal Saudi Air Force, had more powerful engines, improved performance, and more advanced radar, navigation and fire-control equipment. They could attack with collision-course weapons which were heat-seeking and computer-launched after the aircraft had been radar-guided on to its target. By the middle 1960s the security screen which had surrounded the Lightning and its development progress was being relaxed a little. The Lightning, it was revealed, could make a reheat take-off, climb supersonically, and then accelerate to twice the speed of sound in three and a half minutes to intercept hundreds of miles from base. Using the fire-control system, the pilot could make a radar search of the sky ahead, lock on to a selected target, approach under computer-generated steering guidance, and attack with missiles, rockets or gunfire. Infra-red homing missiles, two-inch high-explosive rockets and twin 30mm Aden guns, carried in rapidly-interchangeable, self-contained packs, gave a choice of armament in the interception role, a turn of the pilot's weapon-selector switch being all that was necessary to accommodate the fire-control computer to the change of weapons.

The Red Top collision-course missiles carried by the Lightning as the principal interception weapon could be fired singly or in pairs from above or below the target. The Lightning could be supplied with a powerful ground-attack capability, plus the ability to carry out supersonic high or low-level reconnaissance. A Lightning aircraft already existed which could carry two 1,000lb bombs or rocket launchers delivering a total of 36 SNEB 68mm rockets. A new version that

Above: An impromptu conference of ear-muffed RAF ground crew around No 56 Squadron aircraft on duty in Malta. This night scene was taken in July 1965. / *MoD via A. Price*

Right: No 74 Squadron flew F6s from Tengah, Singapore, from June 1967 to August 1971, when the aircraft were handed over to No 56 Squadron in Cyprus. During their sojourn in Singapore the aircraft, two of which are seen here with overwing tanks, exchanged bases regularly with Royal Australian Air Force Mirages from Butterworth, Malaysia. / *MoD via M. Hooks*

was currently on the drawing boards, but likely to be translated into hardware quite soon, could carry up to six 1,000lb bombs or 144 SNEB rockets in eight launchers, in addition to its normal armament of two 30mm cannon and 44 spin-stabilised two-inch rockets in a special fuselage pack.

Reconnaissance facilities were also provided by changing the fuselage rocket pack for a five-camera reconnaissance pod for high or low-level reconnaissance. Interest in this new version was being shown by countries in the Middle East, as well as air forces in many other areas of the world, it was said. The ground-attack facilities which were being offered by BAC for the Lightning enabled it to carry more than 400 different combinations of stores, including high-explosive bombs, fire bombs, rockets and reconnaissance packs. Six 1,000lb bombs could be carried, four on underwing pylons and two on overwing attachments. Alternatively, the two overwing positions could each carry two Matra rocket launchers carrying a total of 72 SNEB rockets and four 1,000lb bombs retained under the wings.

Another alternative would be eight rocket launchers

carrying a total of 144 rockets. All these combinations made the Lightning, 'a veritable flying armoury'. Although the Lightning was designed primarily as a high-flying interceptor, its basic characteristics of sturdy airframe, good fatigue life, and docile behaviour in the more turbulent weather encountered in low-level sorties enabled it to adapt readily to its new role. All pilots who had flown the Lightning had commented enthusiastically on its docile handling and accurate response to the controls. These two characteristics gave the aircraft a big advantage when used in the ground-attack role. The Lightning also benefited from its ability to use its radar and built-in computer to work out optimum weapon-release points during ground-attack sorties. All the pilot had to do was to approach his target and track it with an aiming mark projected on to his cockpit weapons sight. Radar and computer then combined to work out and signal the optimum firing point to the pilot. The system was easy to use and very accurate.

The Cockpit View

Wg Cdr Beamont, chief test pilot of English Electric, had lived with the new project from its earliest days. He recalled:

'In 1948, English Electric were developing the first jet bomber, and the new design team led by Teddy Petter, had got to the point where the design of the Canberra was 90% complete, the first flight of the prototype was in sight, and the young design team were already looking for their next project. In 1947, the then chief scientist and the first Labour Government issued a considered statement that supersonic aviation was not for the British. It was too costly and too dangerous, and all the necessary research could be done by models. Teddy Petter and his men said "nuts" to that.

'They reasoned that this sort of research could not be done with models, whatever Farnborough thought, it was not too costly, that supersonics were the way to the future, that Britain must be in on it, and that they could do it. They produced design studies for a supersonic research aeroplane using all known techniques and off-the-shelf engines. It was a basic vehicle which could, hopefully, be developed into a fighter. Petter lobbied the Air Ministry to get the airmen on his side. Airmen are very seldom short of enthusiasm, and at least some of the air marshals bought the idea, and so did some of the engineers in the Ministry of Supply, and at Farnborough. By 1948, English Electric had put forward a design study for a prototype — one aircraft and a structural test airframe. The ministry re-wrote around this a fighter requirement F23/49 for a prototype vehicle with two axial-flow engines — Sapphires — with no exotic developments like re-heat, and this was targeted to have a maximum speed of Mach 1.2, fighter manoeuvrability and strength, and a basic armament of guns.

Right: XA847, the first prototype P1B slants down, airbrakes out, across the English Electric factory towards the Warton runway. / *BAe via R. P. Beamont*

'The specification was issued and a contract was placed with English Electric to build two prototypes and a test airframe — the first supersonic contract to be placed in the UK. In the meantime, Hawkers and Vickers were testing subsonic prototypes which were to become the Hunter and the Swift and were having problems up against the sound barrier largely because they were aircraft which were not designed for supersonic flight. The P1 was designed to operate normally at supersonic speeds; it was in parallel at that moment with two other supersonic projects, the Espadon, in France, and the F-100 in the United States. All this was causing a great deal of interest at Warton where Dai Ellis set up a supersonic wind tunnel, and where we had a team of real experts. We were alll pretty young and experienced in our own professions and with most of our careers in front of us.

'Before we got to 1954 and first flight, the Air Ministry became so enthusiastic that they said they would go ahead, without seeing the flying vehicle, with an order for the P1B, the fighter variant of the P1 (the

P1A was the second P1 to fly, and was the one with guns; the P1B was the full fighter vehicle with nearly double the power; the P1 was designed for Mach 1.2 and the P1B for Mach 2 plus — all this before first flight and between one prototype and another). It was a breakthrough aircraft, and from my point of view as the pilot, I had to have a degree of confidence in the engineering that was going to build an aeroplane that was going to sustain my person in an area of flight where little was known. Prior to first flight, I was able to go down to Farnborough and fly the first simulator in this country to be developed for a particular aeroplane. It had been developed jointly by English Electric and the RAE.

'We had quite a bit of work to do in establishing parameters for controlling the first aeroplane in this country with irreversible power controls all round. There was a tremendous debate going on in aviation at that time over whether or not there should be conventional "feel" in the controls. I took the view strongly that flying an aeroplane without "feel" would

CHOP THRU CANOPY
FOR EMERGENCY RESCUE

46

be like driving a car with a steering wheel which did not self-centre itself after taking a corner. On the simulator, I started to pick up a fairly good picture of how this breakthrough aeroplane, which after all, had a 60° wingsweep, about twice as much as anything we had seen before, would behave. The aerodynamics and stability were fairly well understood by the experts, but nevertheless, we had no practical experience of it. It

Below left: The P1 was first shown to the press and British public in 1955 when Bee, seen here in the cockpit, flew a demonstration. An unusual hissing noise with which the aircraft filled the airfield after it had passed made headlines in the popular papers as being akin to 'whispering snakes' / *BAe via R. P. Beamont*

Below: Bee in the P1 moves in unusually close on the chase 'plane during the first photo sortie. It was a fine example of what Bee terms 'adjacent photography'. / *BAe via R. P. Beamont*

was going to land very much faster than any aeroplane I had flown before. Overall, it looked like being a very different beast.

'We took it down to Boscombe Down in the spring of 1954 because the runway at Warton at that time was considered by me to be too short, and we got it ready to fly in the early part of August. The first flight on 4 August was unexceptional in that it flew exactly as it was predicted to fly, with one minor exception. We had done runway trials prior to first flight which involved testing the undercarriage system, brakes and tail parachute, and finally making two straight hops, one to test the elevator in the take-off configuration, and the other to get a brief feel for the ailerons. Both of these had been perfect, with no trouble at all. The hops were up to about 10ft for 600-700yd. So in that sense, the aeroplane had already been into the air before first flight; it is a policy which I have always followed in testing a new aeroplane in order to build up confidence in the basic calculations on stability and control, because the moment you get an aeroplane off the

ground, a test pilot can establish whether he has got the right sort of control responses to fly reasonably accurately.

'On the first flight day we had no problems technically; the aeroplane flew extremely well. We did have one operating problem in that in our anxiety to get the flight done after technical delays the previous week, I was perhaps, a little over-confident, or maybe I was not briefed as well as I should have been. There was a bit of cloud about, and after take-off I was joined by a photographic Canberra flown by Peter Hillwood which was to take the usual pictures of undercarriage operation and other items. We met up at 10,000ft as planned in the neighbourhood of Boscombe. After one wide circuit of Boscombe aerodrome carrying out scheduled tests I noticed that the ground was becoming obscured and that some low stratus had blown in. At that critical moment we had a communications breakdown between my aircraft and the chase aircraft and betweeen the chase aircraft and Boscombe.

'We ended up in the classic situation of being out of communication with each other and with the first flight of this new aeroplane taking place out of sight of land, and of radio contact and not being able to get an instant radar steer back to base. By this time my attention had been diverted from testing the aeroplane to watching the weather and I realised that the low stratus was in fact lifted fog running up the valley and it looked as if it might be very difficult to get back underneath. So I had to throw away the rest of the test programme and let down to what I thought was Amesbury. It was, and I came down into the Avon valley beneath very low cloud, which you don't normally do with a new prototype on a first flight and winkled my way back into the Boscombe circuit, where I found the cloudbase was no more than 300ft (I think we've all become a bit more professional since then; we didn't worry too much about the weather at the time; we were ready to fly, and we went and flew).

'However, I was so pleased with the quality of the aeroplane, that having recovered back into the circuit and with a little bit of fuel left, I did a few circuits to show everybody the aeroplane. I had found a slight over-gearing in the lateral control sense, and in turning there was a slight pilot-induced oscillation. We altered the gearing subsequently and solved it. My test schedule had allowed for a practice approach and overshoot, but I was so confident of it by then, and I was under-confident of the existing weather, so that when I found it setting up very nicely on the approach to Boscombe first time, I decided to make that the landing. The aeroplane came in at the prescribed speed with flaps down just as if I had been doing it time and time again. I felt completely at home with it. I brought it over the threshold at about 165kts, which was very fast in those days, and proved to be faster than we needed. I did a touch down which even I was pleased with, a delightfully smooth landing. I streamed the tail parachute and lowered the noesewheel gently on to the runway.

'I was able to report after the flight that apart from the radio failure and the slight over-gearing of the ailerons, I had experienced no technical faults in the control or stability of the aeroplane worth mentioning. After the usual post-flight checks, we flew again two days later. On the first flight we had achieved all the performance test points, in spite of the weather, including 0.8Mach number, 450kts — which was unusual, even by today's standards. So on the second flight we decided we would take 0.9 Mach number up to 30,000ft, the previous best height being 15,000ft on first flight. The weather was nice and we climbed up to 30, the aeroplane showing a very high rate of climb,

Below: P1B, seen here on first flight on 4 April 1957 with Bee at the controls, was a very different aircraft to the experimental P1 and P1A. It had Avon 24R engines with reheat and provision for a full weapons system with Ferranti radar in a new nose. In this picture, Bee has the airbrakes, situated just below where the slope of the fin joins the spine along the top of the fuselage, extended.
/ BAe via R. P. Beamont

WG760, the historic 'grandfather' of all the Lightnings, in which Wing Commander Beamont made the maiden flight from Boscombe Down on 4 August 1954, now stands at the gates of the RAF apprentice college at Henlow where it arrived in June 1967.
/ BAe

cabin pressurisation, engines and systems all functioning well with no warnings, handling excellent, a little bit over-sensitive laterallly, but very good in pitch and directionally — with a long, thin fuselage, we had expected it to be very good.

'At 30,000ft, somewhere off Poole harbour, I levelled out and at full throttle let the aeroplane accelerate. It seeemed to be going so well that I thought, maybe we'll go to Mach 1 today. It didn't go to Mach 1 indicated. It went to 0.98 and after about two minutes it showed no sign of wanting to accelerate above that. To conserve fuel, I throttled back and turned back towards Boscombe for a long, slow descent during which I could carry out a number of other tests on the aeroplane. Back at Boscombe I declared the aeroplane fit for another flight the next day.

'When I came in the next morning, the chief flight test engineer Don Horsfield, who is now chief of aerodynamics at Warton, said, 'Got news for you Bee. You did Mach 1 yesterday'. They had checked the records from the instrumentation, calculated the instrument error and the position error and shown that 0.98 indicated had just about nudged Mach 1. It was all innocuous. The aeroplane had behaved beautifully, and we decided on the basis of that that we would put it supersonic next time following the same flight plan, climbing to 32,000ft over Swanage and turning up Channel over the Isle of Wight. We held maximum power for about three and a half minutes and the Mach meter which had held steady at 0.98 for about a minute suddenly swung up to 1.05. We were fully supersonic in level flight and this was the first British aeroplane to do this. There was just enough fuel in this fuel-limited prototype at that point to check the control responses in pitch and in yaw, and although one could tell the difference between subsonic and supersonic there was no deterioration in controlability. The aeroplane felt absolutely smooth, responsive and confidence-making. I began to feel that I wasn't sitting in a prototype, research aeroplane so much as a real potential fighter.

'Again, a left turn somewhere over Chichester Harbour, which I remember, because it was strange to be sitting in this new research aircraft and looking down at my old home and the harbour where I used to sail as a boy. And then back down towards Boscombe. This was right at the beginningof the supersonic era. The sonic boom was news, and although it wasn't exactly encouraged, and later became strictly illegal, I thought that all the hard-working characters at Boscombe Down would welcome some indication of what was going on. And so I let the nose down gently 30 miles short of Boscombe, aimed it at the centre of the airfield, increased the power slightly, the Mach meter rose above Mach 1 again, and they knew that the P1 had gone supersonic before I landed. In three flights we had gone through supersonic speed, which was a tremendous rate of progress.

'It flew extremely well — looking back, better than any other prototype I have ever flown. We weren't getting any snags on it, and from then on we flew the aeroplane very hard, accumulating something like 14 short flights before the end of the August, in the hope that we would be permitted to fly it at the Farnborough show in September. However, we had not got the mandatory ten hours in that 14 flights. When the Farnborough period came up, I was convinced that we had a safe, good aeroplane which we could demonstrate at low level in display. However, the authorities quite rightly stuck to the rule that a prototype aeroplane must have had 10 hours' testing behind it. And so we weren't able to go to Farnborough, and I had the interesting experience that week of sometimes flying over Farnborough in the P1 while the display was going on and listening to my test pilot colleagues calling on their radios while they were doing their displays at Farnborough.

'During the week I went back to Farnborough from Boscombe to do the first public demonstration of the latest version of the Canberra, the B8, a low-level interdictor version. I then went back to Boscombe on the P1 programme, and the next target was to clear a specific number of tests which had been deferred for completion before delivering the prototype back to Warton. We completed those in 22 flights by the third week in September, and in flying the aircraft back to Warton, I took the opportunity of taking it close to Mach 1 all the way so that the journey from Farnborough to Warton, a distance of something like 170 nautical miles, was done in $18\frac{1}{2}$ minutes.

'By that time we were satisfied that we had not got a freak experimental aeroplane; that we had got a prototype machine on which we could perform a very high-rate test programme. We had two years to go before the fighter version, the P1B, with a great deal to do. The first thing was to prove the prototype up to Mach 1.2, then go beyond that in two ways, by increasing power and, if necessary, by developing the aerodynamics. In the process of testing it up to 1.2, we found that the directional stability was not adequate to go much faster as the fin wasn't big enough. This had implications for the P1B. Before committing ourselves to the fighter, it was decided to investigate thoroughly the directional stability of the P1 at higher speeds by increasing the power. Thre was no way of increasing the basic engine thrust, and so it was decided to go for a rudimentary form of reheat.

'It would have taken time and considerable cost to develop a variable-nozzle reheat system just of a one-off prototype, and so a simple "blacksmith's system" fixed-nozzle reheat was produced which increased the power of the engine by 10-12%, but reduced the basic dry-thrust of the engine by some 50%. This gave us a no single-engine recover. If we had lost an engine, we could have only done a controlled-energy descent. I accepted this on the basis that it would be a visual-flight situation only. This fixed-nozzle reheat system had the potential of putting the Mach number up to 1.5 or more. The aeroplane responded to thrust exactly as predicted, enabling us to take it in stages up to Mach 1.52. At this point we found that the directional stability had dropped to a level below which I considered it would not be practical to continue testing. At that point we stopped, and the fin size for the Lightning was redefined; but it was subsequently necessary for the fin to go through three further revisions up to its present size. This was the one area where the design of the aeroplane was under-estimated.

'The second prototype P1 flew at the end of 1955, with guns, and with pedal brakes. The first aeroplane flew with conventional British hand-lever brakes, which the British always liked. But about the middle 1950s, it started to be a convention to do it in the American way, because in the view of the RAF, "the Americans did it best". We spent a lot of taxpayers' money putting in pedal brakes. The RAF, when they compared the two, didn't like the pedal brakes as much as they liked their old hand brakes, so they went back to the handbrakes.

'We did the first gun firing with the P1 in 1956, and supersonic gun firing before the end of the programme in 1956-57. We exhausted all the possibilities of the P1, which proved an extremely valuable test vehicle. The second prototype with guns went to RAE Bedford for low-speed stability and control work. The first prototype stayed with us at Warton for continuation training. We used it for about two years as a back-up so that when our pilots were not getting flights in the Lightning prototypes, they could keep in practice on the P1. Both those aeroplanes are now at the RAF cadet school at Henlow. They were a perfect example of the value of courage and foresight in designing a flying prototype to see if theories are right, before committing vast sums of taxpayers' money on a whole production run of aeroplanes.

Below: The ultimate Lightning, the Mark 6 (this is the first production aircraft) out on test from Warton in the hands of Bee in front of a familiar local Lancashire landmark the Blackpool tower and piers. Distinguishing marks are the 'beefed-up' fin and the large ventral pack containing extra fuel and/or a weapons pack in the front sections with twin stabilising fins at the rear. / *BAe via R. P. Beamont*

Above left: In formation as if locked together, four Lightnings of No 23 Squadron give a vivid impression of the power of this classic British fighter. / *BAe*

Left: Three Lightnings follow a Canberra and a pair of Buccaneers across a section of British coastline. / *MoD*

Above: Streaking across a sea of clouds, this No 56 Squadron aircraft sums up the power and purpose of the Lightning in supersonic flight. / *R. J. Wilson*

Right: A contrast in colour schemes. Two No 92 Squadron F2As, the top one in the traditional all-metal finish, the lower with dark green upper surfaces painted while the squadron was serving in Germany. / *Image in Industry —*

53

'That was the last time that we in British aviation have done a pure prototype programme, except perhaps for the Harrier, which was developed from the Kestrel at about the same time as the Lightning. The P1B Lightning, which had its first flight in 1957, had substantially the same aerodynamics, but was re-engined with Avon 24R engines with reheat, and a full weapons system with Ferranti radar. It was another extremely successful prototype. It carried out a large number of flights in the first two months before laying up for engineering work. There were no preliminary hops before the first flight at Warton — just a straight climb to 30,000ft and accelerating to Mach 1.2 This was in dry thrust, and there are very few aeroplanes today which can go supersonic in dry thrust.

'At the beginning of that programme, that aeroplane was the original high-energy fighter. It began its life with a one-to-one thrust ratio, so that once we started to do full reheat climbs, it was a most spectacular experience. It was unusual, in 1957, to say the least, to have an aeroplane which could climb from brakes-off to 30,000ft in two and a half minutes. The Lightning was a long programme. It went through more than 20 prototype and development aircraft types. In the planning, it was decided that this was to be the air force's major fighter development programme for the 1960s, and that nothing must be spared.

'There was a great deal of enthusiasm, but as is common to all fields of human endeavour, some things were not quite right in the planning. People were over-optimistic in thinking you were going to save any time at all in a development aircraft programme with 20 aeroplanes. The net result was that as we got more than ten or 12 aeroplanes, even though some of them were fed out to the Service test establishments, Warton had to give engineering support wherever the aeroplanes were. With rectifications, modifications, and normal servicing lay-ups, the whole thing backed up until we ended up with a grounded fleet. This was a major administrative problem requiring major and immediate drastic action. From it we learned that one development organisation can manage, from one base, five or six prototypes cost-effectively, but that if you are going to have a programme with 10 or more development aeroplanes, that programme has to be spread over a number of bases, each of which must be equally equipped to support its four or five machines.

'We learned the hard way on the Lightning, and this resulted in a delay of a year into service. It should have gone into service in the second half of 1959; it didn't make it until the end of 1960. Nevertheless, it was a great achievement, because it was still a $3\frac{1}{2}$-4-year programme from first flight to service with No 74 Squadron, with a Mach 2 capability, radar, missiles, fighter. The development programme was massive, with prototypes for stability and control, engine development, avionics, gun-firing, missile-firing, development of the radar and the displays. There was a prototype for every part of the job, including one for spinning, with an anti-spin parachute, and we base all our programmes today on this general mangement principle. The Tornado programme, for instance is based on 13 flight development vehicles spread over three bases.

'We were required to clear the Lightning for Mach 1.7 into service with the RAF, and that was done with a great deal of comfort. In fact, we tested the aeroplane to its service release speed during the initial handling period within six weeks of first flight. Having done that, it became very apparent that there remained an impressive excess of thrust over drag.

'The classic thrust equals drag flat curve for a supersonic aeroplane in standard conditions was reached in theory at something in excess of Mach 2.2 for the Lightning and so at the end of 1958 I started going through with the performance department what were the obstacles in taking the aircraft beyond 1.7. Freddie Page, as the chap carrying the can, was less interested in jumping ahead until we had proved what we had got to prove for entry into service. But he has always been prepared to have a go and he eventually said, "Don't get your priorities wrong, but if the circumstances are right, use your judgement and I'll support it."

'One day in October 1958, I went off in the first prototype XA847 with two test schedules down to Colwyn Bay to accelerate up the Irish Sea. The normal schedule required some stabilised performance measurements. But if the tropopause temperature and height were right, and if the conditions were non-turbulent, and the visibility was good enough so that I didn't have to worry about close radar control, I was going to decide to throw the first schedule away and use the second schedule, which was for an acceleration to Mach 2. We had reached 1.8 and 1.9 in the previous weeks. I realised on the climb that conditions were going to be better than forecast. I went on the radio and said, "Schedule two", and set off on the Mach 2 acceleration.

'We expected starting from Great Orme Head to reach Mach 2 on full-power acceleration but had already reached 2.0 when level with Douglas IOM. With the Dumfrieshire coastline looming up fast ahead, I turned starboard to decelerate over the Lake District on that occasion, which must have caused a lot of boom. The run was absolutely trouble-free, but what we were looking for was two things — one, possible deterioration of directional stability at upwards of 1.8 and, two, intake surge, or buzz, which we thought would be much more likely. This was a pitot intake designed to have its maximum efficiency at around 1.7. The pessimists suggested that we might run into fixed-throttle buzz at around 1.98, or if we didn't, but pulled any G there, we would pull straight into the buzz.

'When it occurred, it would probably be like a continuous explosion right under your feet, and the pessimistic assessment was that if it was allowed to continue for any length of time, it would fatigue the duct, and you would end up with the engine digesting a lot of intake. But like so many things in this programme, the experts knew exactly what they were predicting. They were putting pessimistic margins on for the sake of safety and my health, which I appreciated. But the aeroplane proved better than the worst estimates, so that we got to Mach 2 without problems. Just as we reached Mach 2 at 41,000ft, I was conscious of an abrupt rise in noise level under my feet which, when we looked at it, was the beginning of the first signs of buzz, but it never reached serious proportions. I pulled a starboard turn of 2G to see if it would increase the buzz level, and this confirmed to me that what I was feeling was this intake buzz.

'The aeroplane responded beautifully at Mach 2. It was still directionally stable, even though we hadn't got auto-stabilisation. It was a basic aeroplane. I then throttled back, encompassing almost the whole of the Lake District in a decelerating starboard turn, and then drifted off back home at Mach 0.9 with the aeroplane in perfect shape. The other point which we had been concerned about was temperature. The ram temperature at the cockpit at Mach 2 was estimated to be as high as 120°C. At 135°C, plus, we could expect deformation of the transparencies by thermal distortions which could have caused the cockpit canopy to come off. In fact before doing this, I had taken the precaution of getting a ram temperature sensor with the gauge rigged up right in front of me on the coaming, and we saw 115°C on that.

'So we returned back to base, with the RAF's first potential Mach 2 fighter. As a result of that I wrote a report to the various ministries concerned saying that that flight and the previous work-up flights proved that we had in the Lightning a potential Mach 2 operating aeroplane which could provide that facility for the Service once it had been developed in terms of fuel capacity, for the initial Lightning was a very short-range aeroplane, designed to defend the east coast V-bomber bases with only a 150-mile radius of action.

'This very strictly limited its operational capability, and it was quite apparent that if you were going to make use of its potential as a Mach 2 fighter, you had got to put a lot more fuel in it. I wrote at the time that we needed to double the fuel capacity, but nothing much happened, although a great deal of discussion and debate went on. Then in 1963, the ministry decided that they wanted to increase the range capability of their Lightning force. They instructed the

development by English Electric/BAC of a revised fuel system for the Lightning incorporating a much larger ventral tank, which resulted in the Mark 6 Lightning, which had double the fuel capacity of the Marks 1 and 2.

'This became the aircraft which was the basis of the successful order for Saudi Arabia and also for the fighter defence of the UK with the Lightning, and for the 2nd Tactical Air Force in Germany, which had the original Mark 2 Lightnings re-worked by the manufacturers to incorporate the increased fuel system. The path to all that was strewn with development problems common to any aircraft which incorporates high technology, particularly the weapons system, the AI23, which was eventually raised to a very good standard, and the airframe itself — we lost two fins in development — Johnny Squier falling into the sea in the first prototype T4 trainer and Jimmy Dell doing likewise with the first prototype T5 trainer.

'We also lost aircraft with undercarriage failure, but in the whole programme the problems which we encountered were no greater than in any other programme of a similar nature. In terms of performance and general air vehicle capability, we had no other problems at all. The aeroplane met its specified drag and performance, and you could sum up the programme by saying that the aero-dynamicists got the Lightning absolutely right, but the systems engineering took a bit of time. Politics always enter when big money is involved, and so it enters into aircraft programmes.

'The Lightning was developed for a specific home-defence role, and therefore had a very limited specification. This meant that no foreign buyers had the slightest interest in it at first. Once it was realised that the aeroplane had capability of stretch in terms of fuel it became apparent that it was a very adaptable air vehicle. One of the features of the Lightning has always been that in spite of its tremendous performance, it is a pilot's aeroplane through and through. It has never presented any problem in flying training or operating. Pilots go on to Lightning training, and they just love it.

'Therefore there were not going to be any difficulties in training on the Lightning that were going to be costly. There is already the ability to carry an advanced weapons system to Mach 2, but what was needed was to take the aeroplane over much greater ranges than it was originally capable of. The RAF first said they would do it by flight-refuelling, having a good tanker fleet, and so this facility was developed, very successfully, and all the short-range Lightning squadrons took part in ferrying aircraft as far as Singapore and so on. But what was necessary to make it a flexible aeroplane was the introduction of greater fuel capacity.

Although pugnacious in appearance, the Lightning can also be a graceful aircraft, as this shot of No 23 Squadron aircraft captured above a sea of colourful clouds, proves. / *BAe*

'We put forward from the company, formally, a plan for doubling the internal fuel by retrofit of existing aeroplanes and introduction into new build, before the end of 1960. The Air Ministry we knew wanted to have this incorporated, but there was no decision in favour at that time, I suppose for budgetary reasons. The air force got the whole of its Mark 1, 1A, 2 and 3 Lightning build with the limited fuel system and the Mark 3 had advanced radar with avionics for auto-attack. The auto-attack system was the first in the country, similar to the system in the American F-106, but rather more effective, we believed. It was supremely successful in development. It worked absolutely like a charm. We delivered it up to the ministry on a plate and said, "When would you like to have it?", and they said that by this time (in the mid-1960s) they had found the Lightning so easy to operate manually that they didn't need the automatic attack system!

'Then in 1963 the fuel system development came back to us as a ministry requirement that the Mark 3 Lightning force, which by that time had been built and delivered, was to be retrofitted at the factory with the new fuel system, and they and all later-build Lightnings which would incorporate the new fuel system would be called the Mark 6. Immediately this new fuel capacity became visible, and this is no coincidence I'm sure, the Saudi Government began to show interest in the Lightning. Hitherto there had been

no interest in it from anywhere in the world, barring just passing glances, but the Saudis started to be interested, and in 1965 they placed an order which was worth £85m, and which was subsequently followed up by massive support contracts which totalled something like £1,000m by 1978, all on the basis of the original Lightning order.

'The year 1958 was a time when Europe was looking for a supersonic fighter, and the Americans were pushing to get the F-104 in. The Americans, having laid down very large procurements of the aircraft in advance of flight testing for the USAF then discovered very considerable operating limitations of the aircraft and cancelled all but a few hundred of their own build, leaving a production situation ripe for offering to the world, which they did with all their power of American salesmanship. In this period, there was a competition going on in Bonn. West Germany was seen as the key in the European competition for a fighter. Their purchase would be followed, in the interests of standardisation and convenience, by a number of other NATO air forces.

'We believed that the Lightning had the capability to take a strong part in this competition, and we believed it even more when we learned that the main aircraft in the competition was the F-104, because although we knew this was a capable machine for getting to Mach 2, we also knew that it had very severe operational limitations. One of the reasons was

because I had been over to America and flown it. We sent a high-powered team to Bonn, but it became apparent after a period that we weren't talking at the right government level. We couldn't understand why we weren't getting to the right ministers.

'Then it was revealed in the course of time that we weren't getting there because HMG had let it be known in Bonn that they were not recommending further discussion with English Electric on the Lightning, as it was not considered suitable to the German requirement. At that time there was an aeroplane called the Saunders Roe rocket fighter, which was a ministry procurement which went sour. The Saunders Roe factory was set up to build this aeroplane for the RAF, but the air force did not want it on technical grounds. A strong government effort

Below left: More adjacent photography. Bee tucks in really close in the Mark 6 prototype to the chase 'plane somewhere over the hills of the Lake District. / *BAe via R. P. Beamont*

Right: A two-seater version of the Lightning was not long coming and was a relatively straightforward modification. Here Bee climbs aboard the first T4 before ferrying it from Warton to Boscombe Down in 1959. / *BAe via R. P. Beamont*

Below: XL628, the T4 prototype on its first flight out of Warton. / *BAe via R. P. Beamont*

Left: An F1A of No 56 Squadron demonstrates the Lightning's phenomenal rate of climb, given as an initial 50,000ft per minute, as it stands on its tail. The aircraft is in the striking colours of the Firebirds, the 1963 Fighter Command aerobatic team. / *R. J. Wilson*

Top: Two Royal Saudi Air Force Mark 53 single-seaters bank across the coastline of their desert homeland. / *BAe*

Above: Reflections on a rainy day of No 74 Squadron Mark 3s armed with Firestreak missiles. No 74 was the first squadron to be equipped with the F3 and from 1965 on was frequently engaged in turning back Soviet reconnaissance aircraft from British shores. / *BAe*

61

developed to sell it to Germany in order to maintain employment in the Isle of Wight. This was a technical non-starter in the biggest possible way for anybody who knew about it. There was no doubt at all that HMG defeated any chances of getting the Lightning into that competition, but we would have only got into the competition with a chance if we had been able to develop the fuel system at that time.

'I believe that a massive opportunity to sell Lightnings all over Europe was lost at that time and that we could have sold half to three-quarters of the total F-104 buy. The F-104 was bought primarily for ground attack in Germany and Italy, but in a number of the smaller air forces it was equally purchased for self-defence. The self-defence capability could have been performed by the Lightning very well indeed, and very much better than the F-104. It is likely that had

Above: The extra width across the cockpit which English Electric had to build in to accommodate two men side by side can be clearly seen in this shot of the maiden flight of the prototype T4 taken from the chase Canberra. / *BAe via R. P. Beamont*

Above right: Closer yet! The T4 prototype, Bee clearly visible through the windscreen, nudges almost into the lap of the photographer. The aircraft, with visual identification on its nose for the benefit of the crowd, and with twin Firestreaks mounted, was en route to the 1959 Farnborough show.
/ *Flight International via R. P. Beamont*

Right: Later marks of Lightning can be readily identified by their larger and squarer fins, the prototype of which, on a Mark 3 development batch aircraft, is here seen on test out of Warton in 1959. / *BAe via R. P. Beamont*

the Lightning been on offer at that time, as many as 500-600 sales would have gone to the Lightning.

'The later buy of Phantoms for the RAF was logical when the Lightning was not subsequently developed further as an advanced weapons system. The Phantom had a second-generation weapons system with a look-down radar capability, and advanced missiles. The Lightning system was never developed after Red Top so that it had a simple look-up system. The Phantom look-down system was very much more effective, which isn't necessarily to say that they should have gone for a Phantom purchase without considering the development of a British radar with a look-down capability. With the sort of expenditure which went into the Phantom programme, the Lightning could have been very well developed further. The Mark 6 Lightnings are able to go out 300-400 miles from base and then hook up on tankers, and this is about the same radius on long-range patrol as Phantoms have.

'I went out to Germany in 1977 to see the last Lightning squadrons there before they were withdrawn from 2nd TAF, the policy being to withdraw all remaining usable Lightnings into UK defence, and to concentrate the NATO front line on Phantoms. I was a little unprepared for the reception I got. I found extremely high morale in the Lightning squadrons, who were quite convinced that their role in low-level defence of the front line was being taken over by what they considered was an inferior aeroplane. They reckoned they could outfight the Phantom in any circumstances and at any height. Maybe that they

Left: Trailing wingtip vertices, four Lightnings take up close station. The novel arrangement of their two engines placed one of top of the other is clearly indicated. / *Image in Industry*

Below: XG310, the aircraft testing the Mark 3 fin, Bee at the controls, banks sharply over the north-west England coastline. / *BAe via R. P. Beamont*

were a little biased as keen, high-morale operational pilots. If you pointed out to them that the Phantom had a look-down radar and weapons capability, they asked, "who needs a look-down capability?" The role of defence along the NATO border is on the deck so that you can look up and see what is coming in. They were completely convinced that they had a better aeroplane, more manoeuvrable, quicker reaction that could get off the ground quicker.

'However, the Lightnings went back to the UK, but it now seems possible that they may be kept in service for UK defence until 1990, on the basis that it could be less costly than keeping the Phantoms in service until that date. The argument about fatigue life has now swung away from the Phantom and in favour of the Lightning. What we did with the Lightning was to fund as a nation a major military aircraft programme, producing a vehicle that was without superior anywhere in the world, and then in revival we ran headlong into a number of engineering problems.

'In the early 1960s, those responsible for engineering in the Service undoubtedly said to their lords and masters, this aeroplane is no good, we will never make its systems engineering right. That was said because of a considerable under-estimation of the support task necessary to keep a supersonic aeroplane flying. Once they learned how many man-hours of maintenance you have got to put into a flying hour on a supersonic aeroplane, it all started to come right. Now in the late 1970s if you ask in the RAF at any level about Lightning serviceability, they say, "Old hat, it's marvellous, easy aeroplane, it'll do 45 hours per month per aeroplane any time you like." It was the first of its class, and it was underestimated. But it was that attitude as much as any other factor which prevented it from being funded up for further development, when some engineers lost faith in the Lightning in the early 1960s.'

Supersonic Escape

Mr J. W. C. 'Johnny' Squier was a member of the small and distinguished band of English Electric test pilots who carried out the early flying on the Lightning. On a test sortie in 1959 the prototype which he was flying suffered a major structural failure and he became the first man to bail out safely from an aircraft travelling faster than the speed of sound. This is his story of that day as told to the author in the autumn of 1978:

'The Lightning was a very easy aeroplane to fly. I had one flight in a Hunter to obtain swept-wing experience and, three or four months later, my first flight in the P1. You had a lot of power there, and you were very conscious of the fact that you came off the ground very rapidly. It was one of the few swept-wing aircraft which you could fly quite satisfactorily without auto-stabilisation, and in 140 flights I had been up to 60,000ft and speeds around Mach 1.8.

'On 1 October 1959, I was flying the prototype two-seater on test, doing high Mach number handling at high altitude. The test run which I was using was half way between the Isle of Man and the mainland which gave a long enough run without the sonic boom hitting land. I was doing a high-rate roll, and on stopping there was a bang and the aircraft went out of control. There had been a structural failure.

'The aircraft immediately went out of control, and I did not have time to get a radio call out. I did the only thing I could. I knew I was losing consciousness because of the gyrations of the aircraft and I reached up and pulled the face blind which operated the ejector seat, a Martin-Baker 4BS — the first time it had been pulled at supersonic speeds anywhere in the world. It was a very good example of what happens when you take on a good dollop of adrenalin.

'The time sequence of the canopy and the seat was instantaneous firing of the canopy on pulling the blind, and a one-second delay between the canopy going and the seat firing. If anybody had asked me how long it took for the canopy to come off, I would have said about two minutes and the seat about 20 minutes to fire. This was a worry which has occurred on other ejections when a pilot who has pulled the face blind has had time to pull the other handle because he

assumed that it was not working. The timing was modified later, I believe. You become a superman under these circumstances and do things which are usually impossible to do.

'Having got out of the aircraft, my one instinct was to hang on to the face blind because I was worried about the speed I was doing. I started to rotate rapidly, and the centifugral force pulled my hands off the face blind. My arms were spreadeagled, and I thought I stood a good chance of losing my arms because the pull was so strong and the pain in my shoulders was terrific. The next thing I remember was all being calm and serene. I was in the seat, still slightly face forward. I was just beginning to think that it was time that something happened, then there was a clang and the seat released from me.

'I was not aware of any break in the period, but in actual fact, there had been quite a big break, as I had been unconscious. The seat separated at 10,000ft and at that point the parachute should have opened automatically, but it did not. I was above cloud. I entered cloud and on coming out at the bottom realised that the water was very close. I knew that something had gone wrong, and I used the manual-override handle to open the parachute. It opened immediately. I thought, "Now for a long wait", and I then hit the water. The cloud base was only 1,000ft.

'I went right down. I had not inflated the life preserver, which I should have done. I inflated it under water, and that pulled me back to the surface. I had to get rid of my parachute, inflate the dinghy and get into it. Having done that, my first idea was to get the SARAH beacon working. There was a combined microphone and earpiece, but when I put it to my ear, there was nothing from it. I left it switched on and started bailing out the dinghy. Between one and two hours later an American SA-16 amphibian came over. I fired one of the three pyrotechnics which were in the dinghy, but it did not go off. He went right over me, but did not see me. An hour later he came back. I pulled the pin from another pyrotechnic, but although it hissed, went out without firing. The third one did fire, but by that time the aircraft was over the top of me and he did not see it.

'Later a Meteor came over, and I learned afterwards that the radar station was trying to bring him over the same test route that I had been flying. He was diving through the low cloud, but came down just ahead of me, but he did not see me. Later on, Shackletons started taking part in the search. I could hear them, but they could not see me. I tried to use a heliograph, but it was impossible to direct the sun on to the aircraft. It became dark, and I used the McMurdo light, which is powered by placing its battery in the sea. It was a very nasty night. It was raining, and the sea was pretty rough, and it was an exceedingly long

night. The dinghy top-up valve had been fractured in the ejection, and as the temperature dropped the dinghy became softer. I thought I might have got a leak, and I knew I could not use the pump.

'I became a bit delirious during the night. I dozed off and dreamed that I was on land and finished up not knowing whether I was on land and asleep and dreaming that I was at sea. When dawn broke, I had a swift look round and could see a misty coastline. I pulled in the sea anchor and started to try to paddle with my hands towards the coast. I tried using a knee pad in one hand, but this just resulted in my going round in circles. I then came across a piece of driftwood from an orange box so that I was able to paddle with that and the pad. It took me from dawn until 4pm before I made land. By the time I landed in Wigtown Bay in western Scotland I had been in the water for $28\frac{1}{4}$ hours. I made for a house, following a path through the trees, and arrived in a garden where I found a woman picking roses. She was somewhat startled at my appearance. I said, "I have just come out of the sea." She said, "Stay there. I have read it in the papers".'

Author's note: although, almost 20 years after the incident, the exact nature of the failure is still covered by security, it is generally assumed in aviation circles that the fin failed.

Mr Squier had been given up for lost after his Lightning had hit the sea, and his wife had been told 40 minutes after the crash that there was, 'not much hope'.

Into Service

The Royal Air Force placed its first order for Lightnings — F1s — in November 1956 and, at the same time, put in train a plan to develop a string of airfields running down the eastern side of Britain to take the new aircraft, whose primary role was seen as the defence of the United Kingdom. Runways were extended to 7,500ft plus and many new facilities installed, but the publication of the 1957 White Paper casting grave doubt on the future of manned aircraft stifled much of this expansion. Several of the airfields which were being prepared for the new aircraft were abandoned.

In December 1959, the first F1 was delivered to the Air Fighting Development Squadron at RAF Coltishall, followed by two more in January 1960. For the first time in its history the Service had an aircraft which was able to sustain supersonic level flight. The Lightning was to remain the RAF's only aircraft in this category until the delivery of the first Phantoms from the United States in the middle of 1968. By June 1960, AFDS Coltishall had four Lightnings on its strength and was well advanced in conducting trials of the aircraft and all its systems and working out both training and operating techniques.

No 74 Squadron, the first operational squadron to equip with Lightnings, converted from Hunter F6s in July and August 1960, with the assistance of AFDS. The first aircraft was delivered to No 74 on 29 June of that year. Although there was little time, and the conversion from the Hunter was a demanding task, No 74 squadron flew a formation of four of their brand-new Lightnings on most days of the Farnborough air show in September 1960 (the public had gained their first view of the Lightning at the 1955 Farnborough — the second P1A prototype, flown by Beamont). No 226 OCU, based at Middleton St George, was the third RAF unit to receive the Lightning, taking delivery of their first F1s in July 1963.

Right: The slim lines of the Lightning undercarriage designed to tuck away into the thin wing is very apparent as this Mark 6 moves towards the camera at the 1968 Farnborough show.
/ *Brian M. Service*

Above left: At the British Aircraft Corporation works during a visit, Mark 2A versions of the Lightning from No 19 Squadron RAF, stand on the flight line. / *BAe*

Centre left: By 1958, the P1B development prototypes had sprouted a ventral pod beneath the fuselage with stablising fin and Blue Jay, or Firestreak, missile installations were being tested. / *BAe via R. P. Beamont*

Bottom left: Twenty development batch aircraft were ordered to test all the various areas, from engines to electronics. Unfortunately, the number was too large for the system to manage, and the Lightning was a year late into RAF service as a result. Here Bee carries out a test flight in the first P1B prototype during 1957. / *BAe via R. P. Beamont*

Above: One of the development batch of Mark 1 Lightnings flies in formation with representatives of the aircraft types it was due to replace in the RAF, a Hunter Mark 6 and a Javelin Mark 5. All are from the Air Fighting Development Squadron at the Central Fighter Establishment, RAF Coltishall, in 1960. / *MoD via P. Collins*

F1s were replaced in No 226 OCU by F1As in June 1965, but some F1s soldiered on as target facilities aircraft at Binbrook, Wattisham and Leuchars, acting as 'enemy' intruders on which other Lightnings from the same bases could practise their interceptions. The F1As which displaced them had improvements including a refuelling probe and an ultra high frequency radio. No 56 Squadron began to replace its Hunters with Lightnings on 14 December 1960, when the first F1A was delivered to Wattisham, but No 111 Squadron, on the same airfield, and also flying Hunters followed suit soon after.

Using the new in-flight refuelling capability, there were many practice link-ups with Valiant tankers from RAF Marham, and using the expertise which they had by then gained, No 56 Squadron in July 1962, flew two Lightnings non-stop from their base to Cyprus. It was the first such deployment overseas by the new fighter. No 74 Squadron had formed the RAF's first Lightning aerobatic team in 1962, known as 'The Tigers', but the following year No 56 Squadon formed 'The Firebirds'. They gave many public performances, and a feature of their display was an almost vertical climb immediately after take off which brought home to the watching crowds the immense power which the Lightning packed in its slab-sided fuselage.

Meanwhile, No 111 Squadron had been training in in-flight refuelling and using this technique they flew overseas missions to Germany, Malta and Cyprus. T4 two-seat trainers, 20 of which were ordered (an original order for 30 being reduced) made their first appearance in the RAF on 27 June 1962, at the Lightning Conversion Squadron at Middleton St George. While the RAF gained the measure of the Lightning, the rule was that only pilots with 1,000 hours' of flying experience were accepted for conversion on to it, but when it was clear that the aircraft had no real vices and that it was, in fact, safer to fly than some subsonic types with which the Service had had to cope in the past, young men with only 450 hours were taken on. They usually did some 60 hours of flying and a lot more in Lightning flight simulators before being posted to a squadron where they would do several months 'on probation' before being passed out as a fully operational squadron member.

By October 1964 there were six squadrons equipped with Lightnings, Nos 19, 23, 56, 74, 92 and 111, and the AFDS. The first F2 Lightning went to the AFDS at Binbrook in November 1962. It was an improved version of the F1A, with fully variable reheat in place of four-stage reheat, improved electronics which gave a better all-weather capability, automatic flight control, and a liquid oxygen system. Nos 19 and 92 Squadrons operated F2s regularly, No 19 receiving the first aircraft on 17 December 1962. After taking part in refuelling trials with Victor tankers in 1965, No 19 moved to Germany in September and 92 followed in December.

The F3 Lightning which was next into RAF service could be termed the first of the 'second-generation' marks. It had the de Havilland Red Top missile and the improved A123 Ferranti Airpass airborne interception radar, the two together comprising a

vastly better weapons system which meant that the Lightning could now make attacks from abeam of its quarry rather than relying on pursuit tactics as dictated by the heat-seeking Firestreak missile. To compensate for the carrying of the bigger Red Tops, the fin area of the F3 was raised by 15% which gave the fin a square-cut shape not found on earlier marks. AFDS received the first RAF F3 at Binbrook on 1 January 1964, and No 74 Squadron commenced re-equipping with this type on 14 April that year. No 23 Squadron exchanged their Javelins for F3s from September of that year. Nos 56 and 111 Squadrons began to re-equip with F3s in December 1964, and February 1965, respectively, and a few months after receiving their new aircraft No 111 formed a 12-strong aerobatic team whose performances became well known up and down the country that summer.

In 1966, the true worth of the Lightning as a high-performance interceptor in the defence of Britain was demonstrated regularly when Soviet reconnaissance

Top: Originally classified, this photograph gave the first public view of the sort of weapons which were to be carried by the export version of the fighter, right, the Red Top missile pack, left, the Firestreak missile pack and on the wings two 1,000lb bombs. On the wing in the background is a display mock-up of a proposed twin Matra rocket launcher. / *BAe via R. P. Beamont*

Above: A Mark 3 gives the camera a plan view of its armament of two Red Top missiles which, English Electric informed potential Lightning customers, permitted collision-course attacks. Red Top was, 'highly manoeuvrable and had a longer-burning, more powerful motor than the Firestreak missile, which was designed for pursuit-course attacks'. / *BAe*

bombers began probing the country's radar network (see Quick Reaction Alert). No 56 Squadron flew to a permanent posting on Cyprus in the spring of 1967, the advance party arriving there on 11 April.

A two-seat version of the F3, coded the T5, arrived for the first time at No 226 OCU on 20 April 1965, and this type was used for converting pilots to either F3s or F6s although, like the T4 trainer, it was always

considered as an operational aircraft in case of an emergency. As is recorded in a previous chapter, the developed F3 was also designated the F6, the new version having a greatly-enlarged ventral tank, plus provision for two overwing fuel tanks, so meeting the demand of the customer for greater range, in particular for ferrying to overseas bases. Some of the early F3s were brought up to F6 standard, and later production aircraft were built to the F6 specification. AFDS at Binbrook took delivery of the first F6 on 16 November 1965, but No 5 Squadron was the first operational squadron to convert on to it.

No 5 first operated a Hunter 7A fitted with the instrumentation of the Lightning F6, but took delivery of its first F6s (originally F3s) in December 1965. No 74 Squadron at Leuchars began to replace its F3s with F6s in August the following year and the following months saw an intensive programme of in-flight refuelling practice, culminating in a non-stop flight to Cyprus employing overwing tanks, each of

Top: An impressive array of weaponry hardware laid out in front of this export Mark 53 includes Red Top and Firestreak missiles, Aden cannon, 1,000lb bombs, and Matra rocket launchers. / *BAe*

Above: A close up of a Mark 53 showing twin retractable launchers carrying a total of 44 two-inch rockets which are fitted in place of Red Top or Firestreak missile packs. The rockets are spin-stabilised and are designed to fire with optimum dispersion for hitting the target. Two are fired in 'ripple' salvoes every 25 miliseconds either first from one and then the other launcher, or from both at the same time. The launchers themselves automatically extend outwards and downwards in one second for firing and close again after attack. / *BAe*

which carried 260gal, and rendezvous with tankers. Warton was the scene during early 1967, of successful trials of an arrester hook fitted under the fuselage of the F6 designed by BAC to engage wires stretched across the runways of Lightning bases.

The most ambitious in-flight refuelling exercise in

73

the history of the Lightning began in June 1967, when 13 F6s of No 74 Squadron were transferred from Leuchars to Singapore. Using the greater range of their new aircraft, in-flight refuelling, and three stops on the way, No 74 Squadron reported themselves operational at Tengah air base, Singapore, only five days after leaving Scotland. It was a magnificent example of how, in time of an international emergency, the RAF could mount a long-range back-up operation, and justification of the views of all those in both BAC and the RAF who had for long seen the Lightning as something more than a short-dash interceptor.

The lesson was pushed home even further in the following months with a series of impressive in-flight refuelling demonstrations, among them the non-stop flight of four F6s from No 5 Squadron between Binbrook and Bahrain, and a non-stop flight by two F6s of No 23 Squadron between Leuchars and Toronto for an air show in that city. Yet another version of the Lightning was to follow, the F2A, which was an updated version of the F2 including a selection of the advanced features of the F6, notably the large ventral fuel tank, the wing with the extended camber, and the larger-area fin. Nos 19 and 92 Squadrons exchanged their F2s for F2As during the period encompassing 1968-69. This was the peak period for Lightning service when the RAF had nine squadrons in service, Nos 5, 11 and 29 joining those listed earlier.

As late as 1976 two Lightning squadrons, Nos 19 and 92, were stationed at Gütersloh, in Western Germany, 80 miles from the border with East Germany, as part of the RAF contribution to the Second Allied Tactical Air Force, a major element in NATO's European line of defence. Both squadrons were flying F2As and were outperforming all-comers in the quick reaction, low-to-medium level, visual-interception role which was, and still is, so crucial at NATO's most forward point of air defence against possible attack from the East. The 30 Lightnings of Nos 19 and 92 Squadrons had the task of defending the integrity of the airspace of the northern half of the Federal Republic of Germany and of policing the buffer zone, the 30-mile wide sterile strip between east and west into which no Allied aircraft is allowed to fly so that any airborne presence is at once detected.

The responsibility also covered, jointly with the United States and French air forces, and in liaison with NATO, the maintenance of access to Berlin through the three air corridors available to the west. Rapid, positive, visual identification of what was causing any blip on the radar constantly scanning the buffer zone was the task of the Lightnings. It was one for which they were particularly suited, with their very quick scramble time, rapid climb, fast acceleration to high speed, and outstanding manoeuvrability. For this duty, two aircraft, known to NATO as the Interceptor Alert Force, stood continuously poised, night and day, in quick-reaction hangars adjacent to the main runway at Gütersloh, ready for immediate take-off for the buffer zone, only two minutes' flying time away, to identify whether the blip was caused by a potential 'hostile', or a straying Allied aircraft in danger of wandering across the border into the skies of the Warsaw Pact.

The Gütersloh Lightning crews, both ground and air, constantly rehearsed operations under the conditons of nuclear and chemical warfare. The base is equipped with hardened, bomb-proof aircraft shelters that have power-operated doors of toughened steel, and inside of which the aircraft, equipment, pilots and crews could be concealed until the moment that the aircraft were required to take off. A high level

74

Above left: A further view of the Mark 53 armament mix possibilities. Here the maximum load of 116 Matra rockets are in their launchers and the ammunition for the Aden cannon is laid out in front of the guns. On the left is a pair of Red Top missiles; on the right a pair of Firestreaks; in the centre foreground a five-camera (VINTEN) reconnaissance pack. / *BAe*

Top: Red Top missiles are sensitive enough to home on to the heat from the skin of a fast-moving target and practice frontal attacks have been successfully carried out at closing speeds of Mach 3.5 (around 2,200mph). The ports of the twin Aden guns can be seen in the front portion of the ventral pack. / *BAe*

Above: A close up of a proposed twin Matra rocket launcher. Only a single, 18-rocket launcher was specified by the Royal Saudi Air Force in their Lightning order. Each pair of launchers carries a total of 36 rockets and with the 44 two-inch rockets carried in the fuselage forward weapon bay make the Mark 53 a formidable ground-attack aircraft. / *BAe*

Right: In this split-second camera sequence, a Lightning has just fired one of its missiles which trails smoke from its motor as it pulls away towards the target. The pylons on which the missiles are carried contain ejector charges so that they can be jettisoned in an emergency. / *A. Price*

Top: With the cockpit cover up, an F1A of the Wattisham Target Facilities Flight taxis at Yeovilton in September 1973. A second aircraft shimmers in the heat haze produced by the jet efflux. / *Brian M. Service*

Above: Over the barren Cyprus plain with the snowy Troodos mountains in the background, a No 56 Squadron Lightning climbs out of its base in February 1972. During the Turkish invasion of Cyprus two years later, Lightnings flew armed patrols in defence of the British sovereign base areas on the island, their pilots watching the Turkish fighter-bombers destroying Greek property on the ground. But there were no incursions into the SBA, and no British shots were fired in anger. The aircraft pictured is now in the Saudi training base at Warton, on loan from the RAF. / *MoD via A. Price*

of serviceability was demanded of the Lightning squadrons at this most forward base, and the fact that these targets were met and even exceeded can be seen from the fact that they were flying up to 50 sorties in one day and 500 in a month. One aircraft from No 19 Squadron logged a total of 3,000 flying hours in $12\frac{1}{2}$ years with the squadron. This was equivalent to some four and a half months spent in the air non-stop — representing a notable amount of stress for a supersonic fighter under the arduous conditions of interception service.

The run-down of the Lightning in RAF Service began in August 1971, when No 74 Squadron was disbanded at Singapore as part of the phasing-out of British forces in the Far East theatre. The squadron's

F6s were flown to Cyprus where they were taken on to the strength of No 56 Squadron. Next to go, both in 1974, were Nos 29 and 111, both of which re-formed on Phantoms. No 23 re-formed on Phantoms in 1975, Nos 56 and 92 in 1976, and No 19 in 1977. This left just two squadrons still operating Lightnings, Nos 5 and 11, and as mentioned elsewhere, the RAF plan is to keep them operational until at least the early 1980s, and probably a good deal longer.

Top: Firestreak-armed Lightning F3 XP751/L of No 111 Squadron on the flight line at RAF Wattisham. Note intake cover surrounding nose radome. / *M. Horseman*

Above: Lightning F3 XP765/A of No 29 Squadron at RAF Wattisham. / *M. Horseman*

RAF Lightning Evolution

F Mk 1   First flew 29 October 1959; Into service 29 June 1960 with No 74 Squadron, RAF Coltishall; Out of service November 1974.
Two RR Avon 210 with four stages of reheat
2 × 30mm Aden guns (in fuselage)
2 × Firestreak or 2 × 30mm Aden guns (in removable weapon pack)
Basic Navigation System
Radar A1 23

F Mk 1A   First flew 16 August 1960; Into service 14 December 1960 with No 56 Squadron, RAF Wattisham; Out of service July 1974.
As F1 but with UHF radio, flight refuelling probe, (removable), and external cable ducts (port and stbd)

F Mk 2   First flew 11 July 1961; Into service 17 December 1962 with No 19 Squadron, RAF Leconfield; Out of service May 1974.
Two RR Avon 210 with fully variable reheat
Armament as F1
Very minor differences in appearance to F1A
Navigation System incorporates part of OR.946
Radar A1 23

F Mk 2A   Into service 15 January 1968 with No 19 Squadron, RAF Gutersloh; Out of service April 1974.
Final mark to evolve for service in RAF Germany.
To the F2 as the F6 is to the F3, but without overwing tank facility. Has the large angular fin and may be distinguished from F6 by gun blast tubes below cockpit

F Mk 3   First flew 16 June 1962; Into service 14 April 1964 with No 23 Squadron, RAF Leuchars; Still in service.
Two RR Avon 301(302) with full variable reheat ignited by hot streak from engine
2 × Firestreak or 2 × Red Top (in removable weapon pack)
Full OR.946 Navigation System, with Mk 2 MRG
Radar A1 23B (for Red Top collision course missiles)

T Mk 4   First flew 6 May 1959; Into service 29 June 1962 with OCU, RAF Middleton St George; Out of service April 1977.

Two seat side by side dual control trainer
Two RR Avon 210 with four stages of reheat
Armament as F1A except for upper 30mm Aden guns
Dual control operational trainer for F1, F1A, F2, & F2A
Basic Navigation System
Radar A1 23
Front fuselage 11.5in wider than single seaters

T Mk 5   First flew 29 March 1962; Into service 20 April 1965 with OCU, RAF Coltishall; Still in service.
Operational trainer for F3 and F6 (Retains small ventral tank)

F Mk 6   First flew 17 April 1964; Into service 10 December 1965 with No 5 Squadron, RAF Binbrook; Still in service.
As F3 but longer range
Large ventral tank, overwing tanks for ferrying (removable), cambered leading edge wing, arrestor hook (Later aircraft have two lower 30mm Aden guns in the ventral tank)

Ventral tanks
Small (250gal) jettisonable
Large (610gal) non-jettisonable
Large with guns (535gal) non-jettisonable

Right: One of the early Lightnings produces a spectacular plume of smoke as it runs its Avons up into an engine noise muffler at Boscombe Down. / *MoD via M. Hooks*

A Mind Of Its Own

Among pilots and ground crew, the Lightning gained a reputation as one of those aircraft types with a 'personality' of its own. Certainly, stories about it having a mind of its own are legion. Perhaps two will suffice to illustrate the point. At one Royal Air Force station, the engines of a Lightning were being run up when the machine began to move inexorably forward, nuzzling its way into adjacent buildings. According to eye witnesses, it 'chewed its way into the crew room', so that brick dust and mortar flew out of its jet pipes before ground crew managed to get the beast under control again.

Then there was the quite famous occasion in 1966 on which a Lightning being run up by a ground-staff officer at RAF Lyneham actually took off with the officer on board—to land safely. The officer concerned was Wg Cdr Walter Holden, commanding the maintenace unit at Lyneham, whose previous flying experience was limited to Chipmunks. He was sitting in the cockpit on the runway, but without a canopy, helmet, or armed ejector seat, doing an engine check which involved running them and allowing the aircraft to move a few yards. But the engines apparently went into the reheat phase, with the result that the Lightning surged forward and left the ground.

Emergency calls from the control tower alerted the crash services, and everybody watched and waited for what seemed the inevitable disaster. But Wg Cdr Holden got the aircraft under control. He began to circle the airfield, then made an approach to land. But at a late stage he decided to go round again, and this procedure was repeated three more times while those watching on the ground became more and more tense. On the fourth attempt, Holden landed the Lightning safely with only minor damage to its tailend — a magnificent feat of airmanship.

It is of more than passing interest to note that this aircraft was XM135, a Mark 1, and the first Lightning to go into service with the RAF. It made a total of 1,634 flights during its career with the Service. It was placed in the Imperial War Museum collection at Duxford after its last flight, from RAF Leconfield, on 24 November 1974.

Two other stories are told which reflect the fearsome performance of the Lightning. Off the Scottish coast, the crew of a small trawler were all asleep after casting their nets when a Lightning transited them at sea-level altitude. The impact on the dreaming seamen was akin to that of the last trump, but by the time they had tumbled up on deck to see what it was that had produced this traumatic, end-of-the world thunder, the offending aircraft was over the horizon, and all was serene once more. It was not until several months later during a casual conversation with some RAF men that the skipper of the trawler discovered what had really happened. A similar shock was suffered by the crew of a Russian trawler anchored off RAF Leuchars from where Lightnings used to take off to intercept incoming Soviet reconnaissance aircraft.

The trawler's interest was not in fish, but in listening to and recording on sophisticated electronic equipment RAF transmissions. Discussions went on in the mess at Leuchars for some time on how to get rid of the 'spies', and it was decided that the best way to accomplish this would be to have one of the station's aircraft pay them a visit on the way back from a sortie. A Lightning duly appeared out of the blue at nought feet, and the effect on the Russian operators, hunched over their sensitive apparatus, can only be imagined — like something out of a Bateman cartoon, perhaps, with earphones leaping from heads, eyes goggling, and hair standing on end. What actually happened down below that day will never be known, but it is a fact that soon after the visitation, the Russians pulled up their anchor, sailed off, and were not seen again.

Right: Harry Kerr, a staff photographer of *The Times*, took this fine shot through the bomb aimer's window of a Canberra of a Lightning refuelling from a Victor. / *The Times*

Above: After starting life as a short-dash interceptor for the defence of Britain, the Lightning was accepted by the Ministry of Defence as having a role in the defence of overseas bases. This necessitated lengthy non-stop flights to Malta, Cyprus and Singapore and frequent meetings with the RAF tanker fleet. Here two Mark 3s 'take a drink' from a Victor tanker while the squadron was based at Akrotiri, Cyprus. / *RAF via A. Price*

Left: One of the most amazing aircraft crash pictures ever taken involved this Lightning, one of the development batch of 20, on 13 September 1962, on the edge of the de Havilland airfield at Hatfield, Hertfordshire. The aircraft had been detailed for tests on the missile system, and on this particular day the pilot, George Aird, was on a test flight after an engine change. While on the descent into Hatfield he received a double reheat warning, but as there was no smoke or indications of trouble on any other instruments, he decided to attempt to land. Ten seconds from touch down, the aircraft pitched up out of control, and the pilot ejected only 150ft from the ground. The seat worked perfectly, the parachute deployed, and Mr Aird escaped with his life, although breaking both legs as he plummeted through a greenhouse. An accident investigation found later that a flash fire in the engine bay had weakened a V-screw jack actuating the tail to such an extent that it had failed. / *Syndication International*

Above right: A No 74 Squadron Mark 1 goes past the camera at low level at such speed that it carries ghostly supersonic shockwave patterns with it. The aircraft is armed with Firestreak. / *BAe*

Right: This manufacturers' still publicised the two-seater T4, with the crew in full pressure suits. The trainer, BAC assured, had a performance comparable to the single-seater, with identical equipment, plus duplicated flying and fire controls and instruments. Side-by-side seating was accommodated within a front fuselage only 11½in wider than that of the single-seater aircraft. / *BAe*

A Giant Step

Air Cdre Peter Collins probably knows the Lightning as well as any RAF officer, having been connected with it in one way or another almost without a break from 1959, when as a member of the Central Fighter Establishment team which eased it into service he made his first flight in it, to the end of 1976, when as Officer Commanding RAF Gütersloh, on the central NATO front in Germany, he helped to phase it out of service with the RAF abroad. Air Cdre Collins said that the job of the team at CFE, which was initially headed by Wg Cdr Jimmy Dell, and which included a USAF officer Maj Alvin Moore, on an exchange posting with the RAF, was to assess over two or three years the best operational tactics for this aircraft, with vastly-extended capability, which the RAF were taking on.

It was the RAF's first supersonic fighter with a jump in speed of 100% over anything else they had in service, and a jump in climb performance of considerably more than 100%:

'We found that we were reaching the tropopause in three or four minutes from taking off, even in cold power. If we did a full reheat climb, it was about two minutes to 30,000ft. The Lightning was a giant step forward from the Hunter and the Javelin which were respectively the day fighter and the all-weather interceptor we had in service at that time. It was the first single-seat aircraft which the RAF had brought into service with full all-weather capability, and this aspect had to be looked at very closely to ensure that the work load was one which could be accepted for a single-seat operation, and that the radar system was suitable for the interception problem which we foresaw.

'It has to be remembered that this was a couple of years after the 1957 Defence White Paper which had talked about the ultimate demise of the manned fighter, and no further developments beyond the Lightning, and the impossibility of defending Britain against missile attack which was going to be the major

Right: Displaying its underbelly still left in its original aluminium colour while the upper surfaces are painted dark green, a Mark 2A of No 19 Squadron banks above the German countryside. / *MoD*

threat in the future. The role of the Lightning was seen very much as an airspace policing operation, with the possibility of having to intercept and engage high-flying intruders and of ensuring, if these intruders happened to be bombers, that they did not have the chance of dropping their bombs on this country. It was a reactive defence concept in which the ground radar system was relied upon to pick up what was essentially regarded at that time as a high-flying threat, and the Lightning would then use its exceptionally quick-start, scramble and climb performance to intercept and identify the intruders before they could reach a position where they could carry out an attack.

'The aircraft's climb performance and its ability to accelerate at the tropopause to high supersonic speeds enabled it to use the ground radar information to bring it within range of its own radar, something in the order of 25 miles at that time, and to reach a position from where it could if necessary launch its own weapons. The Lightning had a big performance advantage over the types of aircraft which the Soviet Union were operating in the eastern Atlantic and North Sea areas at that time, the Badgers, Bears and Bisons. Response time of the fighters which the Lightning replaced in RAF service had been insufficient, given the ground radar performance at that time, to prevent a bomber from reaching a position from which it could launch a stand-off missile at Britain. The Lightning certainly closed that gap.

'Its major limitation in those early days was its reliance on what was essentially a pursuit weapon, the Firestreak, which meant that pilots were obliged to go round the back of a target. This prompted the development of Red Top with a forward hemisphere capability, its sensitivity being such that it could "acquire" on the plume of jet efflux from an aircraft from the beam and head-on, or on the kinetic heating of the skin of a supersonic aircraft. In the trials which we carried out, the Lightning did almost everything we wanted it do do, but although the radar was good and

the computer-attack programmes were good, these programmes depended on locking on to the target, and we knew very well that when you locked on to a target, you almost inevitably warned it that you had selected it for attack because radar warning devices were coming into use.

'The advantages of a fully-automated attack programme proved, in operational terms, rather more illusory than real. The pilot still had to do a lot of work, and this work was of a new kind, because the pilot, instead of relying wholly on ground control or on instructions from his navigator to reach a position where he could see his target, now had his own radar, which he had to interpret. In a jamming situation, where ground radar was less able to help him, he was left to work out and implement his own attack path until he decided it was prudent to lock on to the target at a stage when it would not be able to nullify the attack. This introduced for pilots an entirely new art form — the interpretation of radar and the problems of mental trigonometry, which was a very demanding requirement, but gradually as the science of pilot-interpreted radar interception was developed, we provided ourselves with a new expertise, and we developed training methods and instructor skills which we previously had no requirement for. We eventually developed a new instructor category, the IWI, or interceptor weapons instructor, to exploit the Lightning in its all-weather interceptor role.

'During the trials it became obvious that the work load on Lightning pilots was going to prove quite demanding, and we were not able to go along with the theory that they would just lock on and follow the computer programmes. In operational terms, we could see too many counter arguments to this. We saw increasing dependence on the pilot's interpretation of what he saw, and an increasing need for an additionally-competent auto-pilot to free him from flying the aircraft while he grappled with the problems posed by the interception information. The auto-pilot

Above left: No 56 Squadron formed the RAF Fighter Command aerobatic team in 1963, the Firebirds, so named after their phoenix squadron crest. They adopted a vivid colour scheme of bright red on the fin, fuselage spine, and leading edges of wings and tail. Squadron colour schemes generally got out of hand in the two years that followed, and artistic *joie de vivre* was curbed by official word at the end of 1965. / *BAe*

Above: Eleven F6s of No 5 Squadron make their squadron number over Akrotiri, Cyprus. No 5 was the first squadron to receive this version of the Lightning. In two successive years, 1968 and 1969, it won the Dacre Trophy for the top UK fighter squadron in weapons proficiency. / *RAF via A. Price*

Above right: Fourteen Lightnings of No 19 squadron let the world know who they are. No 19 were the first squadron to be issued with the F2 version, and later had the reworked F2A. When they re-equipped with Phantoms in 1977 the squadron had had Lightnings on their inventory for 15 years. / *A. Price*

Centre right above: No 19 Squadron put up 16 Lightnings in a neat box. / *A. Price*

Centre right below: Out of their base at Leconfield, five Lightnings of No 92 Squadron fly in a loose formation past Flamborough Head lighthouse on the Yorkshire coast. No 92 took its first F2s on to the inventory in April 1963. / *R. J. Wilson*

Below: No 226 OCU, Coltishall, Lightnings in an impressive line-up including an F1A and, nearest the camera, a two-seat T4. / *The Times*

was improved and later proved particularly valuable for low-level operations over the sea at night and for intercepting jamming targets.

'The pilot's trade was moved a long way from the day fighter, "up and at 'em" mentality. But as with all operational developments, the pendulum eventually swung the other way. As ground radar capabilities increased and interception techniques improved, better methods of attack were devised and the threat from low level grew. The Lightning had been designed as a UK-based pure interceptor against a high-level, high-performance threat, but we sent it out to Singapore, Cyprus and Germany, and in these overseas environments it was facing a very different kind of threat to the one it was designed to meet, and it was necessary to develop tactics which were threat-

responsive, using the equipment which the aircraft had. The Lightning coped with these new roles very well and proved to be a much more adaptable aircraft than many people had believed. It performed creditably in every operating environment.

'It was always a pilot's aeroplane, very responsive to fly. I have rarely flown an aircraft which gave more pilot satisfaction. It is a very good turning aircraft, which means that it can be used very effectively in the traditional air combat manoeuvres and it had very high potential in the vertical plane. As the tactical situation developed, we realised that the development of the Lightning from its original concept into a pure missile-carrier, which it had become with the Mark 3 versions, was a road which perhaps we should not have taken — that perhaps we should have kept the

Above left: Another Harry Kerr shot, in close up this time, of a Lightning refuelling from a Victor. The Lightning is a Mark 6 with Red Top missiles in place. / *The Times*

Left: A rare picture of a Valiant tanker aircraft refuelling an early Mark 4 Lightning during development trials from Warton. Valiants were withdrawn from service because of structural weaknesses. / *BAe*

Top: Four No 11 Squadron Mark 6s make an impressive sight as they formate against the background of the Forth rail and road bridges. Squadron motto: *Swifter and keener than eagles.* / *MoD via P. Collins*

Above: The dark green camouflage adopted by the squadrons in Germany gave the Lightnings a sinister aspect. Here a No 92 Squadron F2A hurries on a mission above thick cloud cover. / *MoD via A. Price*

guns, and one of the major later developments was to restore the guns. In a close air combat situation you need guns and you are at a disadvantage if your only weapons have a minimum range of release of something approaching a mile.

'On the central front in Germany, the Lightning became almost totally divorced from its original concept for it was rarely able to act as a radar-equipped interceptor or to use its high rate of climb or supersonic performance to any extent. It was more often required to provide defence against low-flying targets, engaging them, almost certainly with it guns, in visual conditions. It is entirely to the credit of the aircraft that it was able to cope very successfully with this new task, and to continue to do so right up to the beginning of 1977 when it was withdrawn from service on the central front. In mock combat with a whole range of aircraft, including Phantoms, Harriers, F-104s and G91s, the Lightning showed up very well.

'The main problem in operations low down was its high fuel consumption. Its turning performance has always been pretty good, and although it is not an ideal aircraft to see out of, the tactics devised for it in the central region were excellent so that the pilots soon became highly skilled at seeing their targets in time to reach an attack position. Its very rapid acceleration made it very difficult to avoid in an intercept situation. After withdrawal from the central region in Germany, there were two Lightning squadrons left in the UK, and their role was to meet the threat to the UK, seen principally as low-level attacks by aircraft such as Fencer and Backfire. But they still retain an ability to intercept high-level aircraft. Up against Backfire, the Lightning could still be expected to give a good account of itself, for although that aircraft is highly supersonic, it would not be expected to be supersonic at low level except in the final stages of an attack. It would therefore be very important to detect it early enough.

'The Lightning has now become part of a highly

integrated defence team of which the major elements are the ground radar system, airborne early warning, and the tanker force. There is no doubt that once the modern threat is detected the Lightning's aerodynamic performance remains entirely adequate to take care of reaching a weapons-launching position. It is still as fast as a Phantom, and it accelerates quicker than a Phantom. Its limitation is in its weapon system and in the number and type of weapons which it carries.'

Below left: Air Commodore Peter Collins before a Mark 3 at Coltishall in 1974 'refreshing' with No 226 OCU prior to taking command of RAF Gütersloh. Note the urging on the engine intake blank to 'Stop FOD' — foreign object damage. / *MoD*

Bottom left: A No 19 Squadron Mark 2A on standby at Gütersloh in November 1972. / *MoD via A. Price*

Below: Mark 2A of No 19 Squadron, with Air Commodore Peter Collins, commanding officer of RAF Gütersloh, makes

acquaintance with the Herman's Denkmal monument. The flight had a special significance in Lightning history, as it marked the 3,000th airframe hour on this aircraft (XN790) and it was flown on 4 August 1975, which was the 21st anniversary of the first flight of the P1. / *MoD*

Bottom: What was known locally as a Kampfgruppe (battle flight) of two Lightnings was kept ready on permanent standby, cockpit hoods raised, Firestreaks in place, in Germany for their air-defence role over the northern part of that country. / *MoD via M. Hooks*

Operation Magic Palm

British Aircraft Corporation won orders in 1966 for 35 Lightning Mark 53s plus seven two-seat Mark 55s from Saudi Arabia and for 12 Mark 53s and two Mark 55s from Kuwait (although additions and replacements brought the total Middle East buy up to 61). The initial purchase was worth some £89m, and in the case of Saudi Arabia, the sale was the cornerstone on which the massive BAC, and now British Aerospace, support operation for the Royal Saudi Air Force was based.

A memorandum of understanding was signed between the Saudi and British governments in 1973 under which BAC undertook ten major tasks in support of the RSAF, and was worth £253m. With the addition of further buys of Strikemaster aircraft, the value of this contract grew to £315m, and then in late 1977 the understanding was extended for a further four years, the value to the British of the extension being £500m. It was at that time Britain's biggest-ever export order.

The story of the Lightning in Saudi service has been a successful one. The aircraft formed the backbone of that country's air-defence force since 1966 when six converted former RAF F2s and T4s were sent out (in an operation known as Magic Carpet) to fill the gap before delivery of the order began, and they will continue in service probably until the middle 1980s until superseded by a force of 60 McDonnell Douglas F-15 Eagles which the RSAF has ordered. The Kuwaiti story is a far less happy one. After operating their aircraft successfully for seven years, that country was then persuaded to buy French Mirages and the Lightning fleet was grounded with inevitable deterioration in their condition in in the fierce heat and sand conditions of the desert environment.

At the centre of the deal which resulted in the sale of the Lightnings to Saudi Arabia was a British businessman, Mr Geoffrey Edwards. In the early 1960s the Saudi regime felt itself threatened by a conflict between Egypt and the Yemen royalists, and

Right: The first Mark 55 trainer for Saudi Arabia comes in to land at Warton airfield after its maiden flight. / *BAe via R. P. Beamont*

they were at the same time beginning to feel the financial power which royalties from their stocks of oil was giving them. American, British and French armaments companies spotted the need and moved in, and Edwards, representing a consortium of British companies formed by BAC, Associated Electrical Industries, and Airwork, bid for the contract to set up the country's air-defence system. From a house which he bought in Jeddah, he established contacts within the Saudi royal family, and when the Labour government came to power in October 1964, soon gained their support for his campaign.

Aggressive opposition from Lockheed, who were offering the Starfighter, Northrop, with the Tiger, and Dassault with the Mirage, was swept aside, among accusation and counter-accusation of bribery and corruption, and in December 1965, Mr John Stonehouse, who was then the British minister in charge of aviation, announced that it was the British consortium offer which had been accepted by the Saudis. There were rumours at the time that the US government had withdrawn their side from the contest as a way of allowing Britain to make foreign dollars with which to pay for their expensive buy of F-111s (later cancelled) which were to replace the cancelled TSR2 project, but any English Electric/BAC man will say if asked that the Lightning sold into Saudi Arabia, and into Kuwait, purely on its performance, which was better than that of any of the other contenders.

The multi-million pound follow-on deals which EE/BAC's successors British Aerospace are still servicing at the time of writing came about when the Saudis discovered the difficulties inherent in a non-industrialised country such as theirs servicing a complex supersonic aircraft such as the Lightning. The May 1973 memorandum of understanding already referred to was produced to overcome these difficulties, and included such tasks for BAC as operating and developing the RSAF training structure for both air and ground crews, maintenance and support of Lightnings and Strikemasters, developing

and operating an efficient procurement and supply system, and the construction and maintenance of buildings and plant. By 1977 there were 2,000 British Aerospace employees in Saudi Arabia. In addition there were 250 workers manning the Saudi defence contract headquarters at Warton, and more than 200 other personnel in the division providing back-up assistance.

Among the many tasks undertaken by this headquarters was the finding of new employees at all levels for service in Saudi Arabia, and the ordering and coordinating of the despatch of products from some 750 companies, most of them British, for use in Saudi Arabia. Such products included aircraft spares, vehicles, air-conditioning units, furniture and office equipment, giving a wide range of British industry new outlets. More than 100 different kinds of specialists and tradesmen were provided by the Warton division in Saudi Arabia, all of them earning high, tax-free salaries. In late 1978, flying instructors were being offered by British Aerospace salaries of £13,353 a year tax free in the first year for working in Saudi Arabia, rising to £16,353 in the fourth year. Flight controller instructors were being offered £8,736 rising to £10,761, also tax free.

Above: The Saudis bought the Lightning because of its enhanced endurance and its performance as a ground-attack aircraft following development of the Mark 6 version. To tide the RSAF over until new-build aircraft began to arrive, they were sent a small number of earlier marks from the RAF, one of which is seen here about to hook up to a Victor tanker. / *BAe*

Left: Two Mark 53 single-seaters of the Royal Saudi Air Force turn over their home base on the edge of the desert. / *BAe*

Above right: Interim-buy Lightnings for the RSAF were coded Mark 52 (converted from Mark 2) for single-seaters and Mark 54 (converted from Mark 4) for the two-seat trainer. Here a Mark 54 refuels from an RAF Victor tanker. / *BAe*

Right: Kuwaiti roundels appear on the wings and the nose of this Mark 55 two-seat Lightning, one of two of this particular version which were bought by that country. / *BAe*

Looking after the 'tail' of the British Aerospace battalions was a massive task in itself. The welfare department attended not only the needs of the 2,000 in Saudi Arabia, but those of their 10,000 or so dependents in the UK. The department had the task of organising movements of personnel between the two ends of the line, making a point of seeing every new employee who went out on to the 'plane in Britain and off it on arrival in the Middle East. The British Aerospace staff were responsible for training up Saudis to wings standard in three years, providing academic, technical and flying instruction at the King Faisal Air Academy, the 'Cranwell' of Saudi Arabia, in Riyadh — the city where BAe's headquarters for the whole operation was sited.

At Dhahran, BAe had two main commitments, the technical studies institute, and the Lightning conversion unit. The institute covers 300 acres or more. Technicians spend one and a half years there being trained after learning English for a year in the English language wing. Then they go to RSAF bases for further 'on-the-job' training. At the Lightning conversion unit, flying refresher training is given to RSAF operational Lightning pilots, and the majority of the flying instructors are RSAF men trained initially at the air academy, and later in Britain, who operated under the supervision of BAe instructors. BAe also provide the staff for an aero-medical centre at Dhahran where physiological training of aircrew, and medical checks on aircrew recruits are carried out.

BAe personnel are also responsible for aircraft maintenance and technical training at two main RSAF bases, producing a high utilisation and excellent maintenance record for the Lightning squadrons. BAe claim that since they took over in Saudi Arabia the state of readiness and serviceability of both Lightnings and Strikemasters has rivalled that of any air forces in the world. Arrival of the Northrop F-5s relieved the RSAF Lightnings of their secondary air-to-ground role, so extending airframe fatigue life and allowing their concentration on air defence and photo-reconnaissance. One of their tasks is to investigate

aircraft crossing Saudi territory unnannounced, and these usually turn out to be transiting airliners whose flight plans have not been filed in advance.

Training on Lightnings is maintained at a high rate. Training sorties often include air 'combat' with F-5s, quick-reaction alerts, during which the scramble time can be as short as two minutes, high and low-altitude reconnaissances, air-to-ground firing practice, and air-to-air firing, using towed targets. The supersonic boom is allowed over the large tracts of desert within the country. RSAF pilots go solo on the Lightning after five hours of dual instruction, plus work on the Lightning flight simulator. Several RSAF pilots have now logged well over 1,000 hours on the type.

It was while in service with the Saudi air force that Lightnings fired their first and, at the time of writing, their only shots in anger. A column of rebels moved against Saudi Arabia from the south. They were halted by other aircraft from the RSAF, and the Lightnings were then sent in to 'soften up' the column as it turned round. So effective were the attacks using two-inch rockets that during the ensuing night the leaders of the invading force sued for peace. The whole operation was judged an immense success and proved that the Lightning would be a fearsome and highly effective weapon in a real war.

The Saudi operation was slightly marred by one incident, but even that had a happy ending. Returning from one of the strikes, one of the Saudi pilots was forced down, ejecting over the vast and inhospitable desert which forms a major part of that country. Before leaving the aircraft, he managed to make a Mayday signal back to base and was told to remain near his parachute as help was on its way. This he sensibly did, while a major rescue operation was mounted. A C-130 Hercules was rapidly put in the air crammed with medics and troops and, escorted by Lightnings, it flew to the crash area. The downed pilot was spotted. While the Lightnings circled overhead, the C-130 was skilfully put down in the desert, the pilot was picked up, and the return was safely made to base.

Far left: All smiles under the wing of the Lightning which he had just demonstrated to the top defence brass of Saudi Arabia in Riyadh in 1964 is Jimmy Dell, the chief test pilot of BAC's Preston Division. The smiles were justified, for a little later the Saudis signed their deal for the aircraft which led to massive support contracts which are still going today. Prince Sultan, the Saudi Minister of Defence, shaking hands with Dell, asked for the demonstration at short notice, and the manufacturers hired back from the RAF an aircraft which happened to be staging through the area at that time. At the special request of the Prince, Dell rattled the windows in Riyadh with a sonic boom. / *Trevor Tarr*

Left: The Mark 53s of the Royal Saudi Air Force over their desert base. / *BAe*

Below left: Three of a (not dissimilar) kind. From front to rear, a Mark 55 two-seater, armed with Firestreak, for the Kuwait Air Force, a Mark 6, with Red Top, for the RAF, and a Mark 53, with

guns, two-inch rockets, and 1,000lb bombs, for the Royal Saudi Air Force, although still in its unpainted form here. / *BAe*

Below: All eyes up as Jimmy Dell demonstrates the Lightning to the Saudi armed forces. Prince Sultan is holding the binoculars. On his right is F. W. Page, of BAC, and next-but-one on the Prince's left is the sales agent, Geoffrey Edwards. Both men played a major part in securing the Lightning deal for Britain. / *Trevor Tarr*

Bottom: A fascinated group of RSAF officers pore over the demonstration Lightning cockpit while the assembled dignitaries are given a conducted tour of the aircraft. / *Trevor Tarr*

Quick Reaction Alert

In a nondescript building near the end of the runway at the Royal Air Force station at Binbrook in the rolling Lincolnshire countryside lies what might be termed the 'sharp end' of Britain's air defences.

The building is the quick reaction alert (QRA) centre, one of a number at RAF bases up and down the country from which is mounted the short-order response by the Service to any threat to the integrity of the nation's airspace.

In RAF terminology it is known as the Q shed, and at Binbrook an undisclosed number of Lightnings, their pilots and their ground crews are on constant 24-hour call there ready to put aircraft into the air within the 10 minutes from callout which the RAF demands.

Binbrook is the base for the two remaining Lightning squadrons in RAF service, Nos 5 and 11, plus a training flight. The squadrons' time from being alerted to leaving the runway can be as little as six minutes.

The Q shed was occupied by No 11 Squadron when I visited the airfield, and a typical series of events leading up to a 'scramble' was demonstrated. Each pilot on Q duty spends 24 hours at a time in the Q shed, which has a lounge and a bedroom for the aircrew, similar facilities for the groundcrew, plus a kitchen where one of the airmen acts as cook. The hangars for the Q Lightnings adjoin these facilities and the aircraft wait in them ready fuelled and armed, and with as many systems warmed up without the engines actually being started.

To pass the hours between alerts, the crews read or watch television, but No 11 Squadron pilots said that they found it difficult to settle down to any activity requiring more than a superficial level of concentration against the knowledge that the alarm could go at any minute. At night, they are allowed to sleep, but sleep can be fitful for the same reason.

Ruling life in the Q shed is a wall-mounted loud-

Right: Doing the job that it was designed for all those years ago, a Mark 6 of No 23 Squadron, armed with Red Top missiles, comes up close alongside a Soviet Bear long-range reconnaissance aircraft to warn it out of British airspace. This picture was taken in 1975 when No 23 were operating out of Leuchars. The squadron converted to Phantoms in October/November of that year. / *MoD*

speaker connected directly to an operational centre at which a constant radar watch, 24 hours each day, 365 days each year, is kept on air traffic over the east coast of Britain. The speaker emits a bleep every 30 seconds to prove that it is live.

A call to action is equally likely at lunch-time or at three o'clock in the morning. When it comes, the duty pilots press a button which alerts the ground crew and run for their machines. Strapped in, they talk to the controller who tells what the Q call is all about. It could be a practice interception of another RAF aircraft acting as 'the enemy', it could be the investigation of what turns out to be an airliner or a light aircraft whose crew has overlooked filling in a flight plan, it could be a directive to fly to the missile ranges in Wales to fire a live Red Top or Firestreak at a Jindivik drone, or it could just be orders to 'shadow

Left: An F2A reworked from the F2, and with all the appearances of a Mark 6, stands ready to scramble in a quick-reaction hangar of No 19 Squadron at Gütersloh. / *MoD*

Below left: Wearing 'hostilities kit' for protection against contamination from nuclear, biological or chemical weapons, RAF ground crews refuel a No 19 Squadron aircraft and rearm its Aden guns and Firestreak missiles during battle exercises at Gütersloh. / *MoD*

Below: To fit their continuing role as a low-level interceptor based in Britain at RAF Binbrook, Lightnings have lost their all-metal finish and are painted grey and green camouflage stripes. The aircraft frequently worked in the late 1970s with the airborne early warning Shackleton aircraft of No 8 Squadron. The picture shows a No 5 Squadron aircraft (nearest the camera), a 'T bird' two-seater, and (top) a No 11 aircraft. / *MoD*

and shepherd' a Soviet reconnaissance machine. For obvious reasons, calls are spasmodic and follow no set pattern. Some pilots have had three in as many days. Others have gone through a three-year tour of duty and have had their only alert on the final day of the tour.

The majority of the juicy 'targets' formed by the Russian aircraft, the Badgers, Bears and Bisons, to give them their NATO code names, go to the Phantoms based in Scotland rather than to the more southerly Lightnings, as the Russians are generally bound for the northern waters, or for the Atlantic. But many of the No 11 Squadron pilots have experienced such intercepts. Almost all of the Soviet aircraft fly quite legally in international airspace, but if they do stray into UK airspace the Lightnings have orders to escort them out again after having formed an opinion as to the intention of the incursion — is he lost, is he probing, is he going to attack or is he, perhaps, defecting? The accepted code of air-to-air signals as laid down by the United Nations aviation body, the International Civil Aviation Organisation, is used to indicate to the intruder that it is time that he 'left the premises'.

The general RAF practice when they find a Russian is to take up station on the port side of the other aircraft so that they can be seen by its captain. Apolitical waves are frequently exchanged between the airmen on either side, while Russian crew members have been known to appear at the observation windows showing vacuum flasks with the implied invitation, 'Would you like a drink?'

A more serious activity on both sides is the taking of photographs with hand-held cameras, and as one Lightning pilot said, 'It often seems like a competition up there to see who can produce the biggest Nikkomat'. What happens to the results of these high-altitude picture sessions when they are returned to base the RAF will not say, but the author speculates that it is unlikely that they are all destined for the squadron scrap book, but rather are analysed by the intelligence branch for any signs of significant changes in the specifications of the Soviet aircraft and their equipment.

But although both sides are generally friendly towards each other when they meet up many miles high over the North Sea, just occasionally a Soviet aircraft banks gently towards its escorting Lightning as a test of RAF alertness and airmanship, while at least one Lightning pilot, concentrating on the tricky business of an intercept on a dark night, had his vision temporarily blinded when the Russians shone their equivalent of an Aldis lamp across the intervening gap between the two aircraft and right into his cockpit.

With the aid of refuelling from tanker aircraft, Lightnings have shadowed and shepherded Soviet aircraft for five or six hours on a single sortie and there is no reason why they should not stay on station, with the aid of regular in-flight 'drinks' for up to nine hours at a time, by which time oil and oxygen are getting low. Pilots said that they do not become bored or tired on such lengthy outings as is frequently the case with airline pilots flying long sectors. This is because there is always plenty to do to keep a single-seat fighter pilot busy. Once or twice, life has been made better still by the potential adversary. Lightning pilots tell the story of how during a shepherding operation one of their number, running low on fuel, called up his attendant tanker on the radio and said, 'I'll have to come for some more gas soon. Where are you?' A voice with the thickest of Russian accents then broke in on the wavelength to give the exact longitude and latitude of the RAF tanker aircraft.

Nos 5 and 11 Squadrons fly a mixture of Mark 6s and the older, shorter-range Mark 3s. Their role, as outlined by the Binbrook station commander, Group Captain Peter Carter, is fourfold — to protect the integrity of UK airspace, to defend the UK in time of emergency, the defence of the fleet, and overseas deployment. This latter role has diminished in recent years, but the squadrons still have regular exchange visits with the French air force and with squadrons from NATO air forces in Europe. The major continuing task is training, and this can take many forms. No 11 Squadron outlined for the author the form that a typical combat air patrol (CAP) exercise could take.

The incoming 'enemy' against which the squadron defends the coast of Britain in such exercises are likely to be RAF Jaguars, Buccaneers or Harriers, coming in low and fast — often not more than a few feet above the sea. The attackers' brief will be to break through to the region of Flamborough Head. That of the Lightnings — on a check ride the squadron would be likely to send up a Mark 3 and its 'T-bird' two-seater — to prevent them from breaking through, flying a CAP pattern up and down the coast some 25 miles offshore.

Being such a 'gas-guzzler', each Lightning is always fully fuelled before departure with 1,200gal. At tactical speeds, each aircraft will burn 20gal a minute, although in the sort of climb for which the aircraft is noted, with full afterburner selected, the rate will escalate to something like 200gal a minute. Pre-flight briefing for the pilots goes into great detail, covering the entire operation, from start-up, taxi-out (not less than 200yd between the aircraft to prevent foreign-object damage), take-off (rotation at 190mph), transit to the CAP area (not below 2,000ft) to avoid annoying the local population, tactics during the CAP operation, and return to base, with instructions about possible diversions.

In transit, the Lightnings will fly in pairs to protect

Above: Leaving its base at Binbrook on a bleak January day in 1978 is a No 5 Squadron Mark 6. / *MoD*

Above right: The fuel tanker is hooked up to this No 11 Squadron aircraft and ground crew carry out routine between-flight checks. / *MoD*

Right: A group of No 11 Squadron Mark 6s revisit the old Lightning base at Leuchars during a tactical fighter meet there in May 1978. / *MoD*

the tail of the other. Arriving on station, they will loiter offshore, partnering each other about a mile apart, the crossover at the top and bottom of the patrol area being so engineered that one pilot always has his eyes to the east from where the threat is expected to come. Much of the advice against the arrival of the 'enemy' is simple fighter-pilot's logic which would be equally understood by those who flew Camels and Spads — use the sun and the clouds, assume that the aircraft you are following has a friend who is about to follow you, watch your tail, watch your tail, watch your tail. Not so comprehensible to the Spad pilot would be the advice to avoid using radar because it gives away the presence of the Lightning through the enemy's tail-warning device (although at certain points in combat it

can be switched on to make the enemy break to order), and to try not to pull more than 6G.

Will the incoming aircraft, whose brief is to represent as closely as possible the tactics of Soviet bombers and fighters-bombers, turn to fight when attacked, or will they press on towards the target? Coming round in a high G turn on the tail of an intruder means covering a wide arc of ground, and even with the high-dash speed of the Lightning a long chase to overhaul him, by which time he could be on his target. And so the Lightning pilots are taught to utilise.to the full the extraordinary performance of their aircraft — climbing fast, and then descending on the adversary, rather than making wide turns. As one No 11 Squadron pilot commented, 'If we use the vertical and the enemy decides to turn and engage, at that point, he is dead.'

What came through very strongly at Binbrook was the immense enthusiasm, even affection, which the men who continue to fly the Lightning have for it. Gp Capt Carter summed it up, and in doing so provided a fitting epilogue for this book on this classic fighter, 'It is still one of the most exhilarating of the high-performance aircraft that are around today. Even though it has a high workload, it is a fine pilot's aeroplane, and everyone enjoys flying it. We may not be as sophisticated as Jaguars and Phantoms, but although some people who are sent here are a little disappointed that they are not going on to the more elegant types, they soon learn to like the Lightning and gain an immense amount of satisfaction from it.'

Note:
It was announced in the House of Commons in late July 1979 — a few days before the 25th anniversary of the first flight of the Lightning — that the Royal Air Force is to form a third squadron of Lightnings to help fill the gap in the air defence of Great Britain until the Tornado comes into service in this role. The new squadron, which at the time of writing was not numbered, will be based with the existing two at RAF Binbrook, Lincolnshire, and is expected to be operational by the summer of 1981.

Below: Still looking very trim and a very potent fighter even though the *marque* began life as a design 30 years previously, Lightnings of No 11 Squadron (nearest the camera) and No 5 Squadron in the spring of 1978. / *MoD*

Right: During the change in 1976 from the traditional all-metal finish to grey and green camouflage, No 5 Squadron Mark 6s were lined up in alternate finishes. Note how the squadron number embraces the squadron crest. The final word on the Lightning top speed as given in the official caption to this picture is 1,520mph. / *MoD*

Below right: A Soviet Bison probing British airspace is kept close company by an F3 of No 74 Squadron out of its base at Leuchars, Scotland. / *MoD via M. Hooks*

Appendices

1 P1 and Lightning Total Build

P1	2 prototypes (P1 and P1A)
P1B	3 prototypes
	20 pre-production aircraft
F Mk 1	19
F Mk 1A	28
F Mk 2	13 (5 converted to F Mk 52s)
F Mk 2A	31
F Mk 3	62 (1 converted to F Mk 53)
T Mk 4	21
T Mk 5	22
F Mk 6	62
F Mk 53	46
F Mk 55	8
Total: 337	

2 Lightning Production

Prototypes *P1* WG760 *P1A* WG763 (Sapphire engines; research aeroplanes) *P1B* XA847 (First British aircraft to fly at Mach 2 on 25 November 1958; now in RAF museum), XA853, XA856 (Avon RA24 engines; intake bullet)

Pre-Production XG307-XG313, XG325-XG333 (all Warton), XG334-XG336 (RAF Coltishall), XG337 (Warton)

F Mark 1 XM134 (Warton), XM135-XM138 (RAF Coltishall with the Air Fighting Development Squadron which later became the Central Fighter Establishment), XM139-XM147, XM163-XM167 (RAF Coltishall with No 74 Squadron. A fatigue specimen, un-numbered, was also built)

F Mark 1A XM169 (Warton), XM170 (set aside for ground training), XM171-XM192, XM213-XM216 (RAF Wattisham with Nos 56 and 111 Squadrons)

F Mark 2 and 2A XN723 (A&AEE Boscombe Down; went to Rolls-Royce, Hucknall for engine development), XN724 (A&AEE Boscombe Down; went to Handling Squadron), XN725 (Warton), XN726 (RAF Binbrook), XN727-XN733 (RAF Leconfield), XN734 (Warton), XN735, XN767-XN770 (RAF Leconfield), XN771-XN773 (RAF Binbrook), XN774-XN776 (RAF Leconfield), XN777 (RAF Binbrook), XN778-XN797 (RAF Leconfield). XN795 was the 'prototype' Mk 2A although it differed from the 2A standard finally adopted. It was subsequently an MoD Tornado flight trials 'chase' aircraft at Warton
Of the Mks 2 and 2A, 15 went to Nos 19 and 92 Squadrons each and the rest to No 33 MU Lyneham, of which five subsequently went to the Royal Saudi Air Force as advance ('Magic Carpet') deliveries prior to delivery of production Mk 53s and 55s. The five were XN729, XN767, XN770, XN796 and XN797. The 31 Mk 2 aircraft following were converted to Mk 2A standard at Warton by a fly-in return-to-works programme from Nos 19 and 92 Squadrons in Germany from 1966 to 1970: XN726-XN728, XN730-XN733, XN735, XN771-XN778, XN780-XN784, XN786-XN793, XN795.
XN725 and XN734 were fitted with Avon R146 engines and a fuel system and equipment as Mk 3 aeroplanes for development flying as 'prototypes'. XN734 was eventually purchased by BAC and used for Saudi project ground training at Warton.

F Mark 3 XP693-XP708, XP735-XP765, XR711-XR721, XR722 ('prototype' Mk 53 for Saudi Arabia), XR748-XR751 (delivered to Nos 74, 56, 111 and 23 Squadrons)

T Mark 4 XL628 (prototype Mk 4; company designation P11), XL629 (eventually went to Empire Test Pilot's School), XM966 (first production trainer; converted to second Mk 5 prototype), XM968-XM972 (RAF Middleton St George), XM973, XM974 (RAF Coltishall), XM987 (RAF Middleton St George), XM988 (RAF Leconfield), XM989 (RAF Wattisham), XM990, XM991 (RAF Middleton St George), XM992 (RAF Wattisham), XM993 (RAF Middleton St George), XM994, XM995 (RAF Leconfield), XM996, XM997 (RAF Middleton St

Right: Five No 5 Squadron F6s in line abreast. / *A. Price*

George) XM989 and XM992 went to Royal Saudi Air Force as Mk 52 'Magic Carpet' deliveries.

T Mark 5 XM967 (prototype Mk 5), XS416-XS423, XS449-XS459, XV328, XV329

F Mark 6 (Delivered to Nos 5, 74, 111 and 56 Squadrons) XR723-XR728, XR747, XR752 (First Mk6 (interim standard) delivered with XR753 to the Air Fighting Development Squadron), XR753, XR754 (First Mk 6 (interim standard) to No 5 Squadron, RAF Binbrook), XR755-XR768 (first 'production' Mk 6 to fly), XR769-XR773, XS893-XS904, XS918-XS932, XS933 (on loan to Saudi Training School, Warton), XS934-XS938

3 Lightning Export Production

'Magic Palm'

Mk 53
Royal Saudi Air Force 53-666 — 53-693, 53-695 — 53-700 (first flight 1 November 1966)
Kuwait Air Force 53-412 — 53-423 (first flight June 1968)
Total 46

Mk 55
Royal Saudi Air Force 55-711 — 55-716 (first flight 3 November 1966)
Kuwait Air Force 55-410 and 55-411 (first flight 24 May 1968)
Total 8

'Magic Carpet'
Mk T54 Royal Saudi Air Force (ex-RAF T4s) 54-650 and 54-651 (Total 2; delivered August 1966)
Mk T52 Royal Saudi Air Force (ex-RAF F2s) 52-655 — 52-659 (Total 5; delivered August 1966)

4 Lightning Final Deliveries

F Mk 1
XM167
RAF Coltishall
26 September 1960

F Mk 1A
XM216
RAF Coltishall
29 August 1961

F Mk 2
XN797
RAF Lyneham
4 October 1963

F Mk 2A
XN788
RAF Germany
22 July 1970

F Mk 3
XR751
RAF Leconfield
16 January 1968

T Mk 4
XM997
RAF Middleton St George
14 January 1963

T Mk 5
XV329
RAF Leconfield
28 February 1967

F Mk 6
XS938
RAF Leuchars
25 August 1967

5 Lightning weights

F Mk 1	(zero fuel)	25,753lb	(1960)
F Mk 1A	(zero fuel)	25,737lb	(1961)
F Mk 3	(zero fuel)	26,905lb	(1964)
F Mk 6	(zero fuel)	28,041lb	(1966)

6 Lightning Basic Data (Export Variants)

Span: 34.83ft (10.62m)
Length: 55.25ft (17.65m)
Height: 19.58ft (5.97m)
Armament: *Interceptor Role*
Two Red Top *or* Two Firestreak missiles
44×2in rockets
Two 30mm Aden cannon with 130 rounds each
Ground-Attack Role